NEW TESTAMENT
EVERYDAY BIBLE STUDIES

NEW TESTAMENT
EVERYDAY BIBLE STUDIES

1 CORINTHIANS

LIVING TOGETHER IN A
CHURCH DIVIDED

SCOT MCKNIGHT

QUESTIONS WRITTEN BY
BECKY CASTLE MILLER

Harper*Christian*
Resources

New Testament Everyday Bible Study Series: 1 Corinthians

© 2024 by Scot McKnight

Published in Grand Rapids, Michigan, by HarperChristian Resources.
HarperChristian Resources is a registered trademark of HarperCollins
Christian Publishing, Inc.

Requests for information should be sent to customercare@harpercollins.com.

ISBN 978-0-310-12943-1 (softcover)
ISBN 978-0-310-12944-8 (ebook)

HarperChristian Resources titles may be purchased in bulk for church,
business, fundraising, or ministry use. For information, please e-mail
ResourceSpecialist@ChurchSource.com.

First Printing February 2024 / Printed in the United States of America

24 25 26 27 28 LBC 5 4 3 2 1

CONTENTS

For Northern MANT 2019

GENERAL INTRODUCTION

C hristians make a claim for the Bible not made of any other book. Or, since the Bible is a library shelf of many authors, it's a claim we make of no other shelf of books. We claim that God worked in each of the authors as they were writing so that what was scratched on papyrus expressed what God wanted communicated to the people of God. Which makes the New Testament (NT) a book unlike any other book. Which is why Christians are reading the NT almost two thousand years later with great delight. These books have the power to instruct us and to rebuke us and to correct us and to train us to walk with God every day. We read these books because God speaks to us in them.

Developing a routine of reading the Bible with an open heart, a receptive mind, and a flexible will is the why of the *New Testament Everyday Bible Studies*. But not every day will be the same. Some days we pause and take it in and other days we stop and repent and lament and open ourselves to God's restoring graces. No one word suffices for what the Bible does to us. In fact, the Bible's view of the Bible can be found by reading Psalm 119, the longest chapter in the Bible with 176 verses! It is a meditation on eight terms for what the Bible is and what the Bible does to those who listen and read it. Its laws (*torah*) instruct us, its laws (*mishpat*) order us, its statutes direct us, its precepts inform us, its decrees guide us, its commands compel us, its words speak to us, and its promises comfort us, and it is no wonder that the author can sum all eight up as the "way" (119:3). Each of those terms still speaks to what happens when we open our minds to the Word of God.

Every day with the Bible then is new because our timeless and timely God communes with us in our daily lives in our world and in our time. Just as God spoke to Jesus in Galilee and Paul in Ephesus and John on Patmos. These various contexts help us hear God in our context so the *New Testament Everyday Bible Studies* will often delve into contexts. Most of us now have a Bible on our devices. We may well have several translations available to us everywhere we go every day. To hear those words, we are summoned by God to open the Bible, to attune our hearts to God, and to listen to what God says. My prayer is that these daily study guides will help each of us become daily Bible readers attentive to the mind of God.

INTRODUCTION:
READING THE BOOK OF
FIRST CORINTHIANS

R eading the Corinthian correspondence requires special sensitivities, so this Introduction is a bit longer than the others in the Everyday Bible Study series. These two letters best fit the common description that reading a letter of Paul is like sitting in a room with someone on the phone when all you hear is one end of the conversation. And these two letters are not even always a conversation!

THE HEART OF PAUL

The Paul of the letters to the Corinthians is a vulnerable Paul with emotions and transparency. Read the following lines, mostly from 2 Corinthians, from Paul carefully. As you do, let your imagination seek an image of his face. What might have it looked like as he said these words, as his words matched his emotions, as he experienced, and then felt about his experiences? You might not be able to resist making the face you imagine he had.

1

To this very hour we go hungry and thirsty, we are in rags, we are brutally treated, we are homeless (1 Corinthians 4:11).

. . . about the troubles we experienced in the province of Asia. We were under great pressure, far beyond our ability to endure, so that we despaired of life itself. Indeed, we felt we had received the sentence of death. But this happened that we might not rely on ourselves but on God, who raises the dead (2 Corinthians 1:8–9).

For I wrote you out of great distress and anguish of heart and with many tears, not to grieve you but to let you know the depth of my love for you. . . . Now when I went to Troas to preach the gospel of Christ and found that the Lord had opened a door for me, I still had no peace of mind, because I did not find my brother Titus there. So I said goodbye to them and went on to Macedonia. (2 Corinthians 2:4, 12–13).

We are hard pressed on every side, but not crushed; perplexed, but not in despair; persecuted, but not abandoned; struck down, but not destroyed (4:8–9).

Make room for us in your hearts (7:2).

Besides everything else, I face daily the pressure of my concern for all the churches. Who is weak, and I do not feel weak? Who is led into sin, and I do not inwardly burn? (11:28–29).

Paul was no stiff. He was an emotional man who cared deeply whether the Corinthians liked him or not. Homeless and without food at times; tested to the limit in confronting a possible martyrdom; full of "distress and anguish of heart and with many tears," unable to preach the gospel because of anxiety over news about the Corinthians, pleading with them to love him and full of pressure about all his churches.

Is this the Paul you know when you think of Paul? Lots of people make disparaging remarks about this man. I suspect they have not read him carefully enough. My own attitude toward Paul mirrors my attitude toward the pastors of our family and churches, the leaders I have known. I respect them; I disagree with them; I get irritated. But I know they love us, they are doing their best, and no pastor and no apostle is perfect. I love Paul, but he's not Jesus.

In these two letters, 1 and 2 Corinthians, you will meet the real Paul. His relationship with the Corinthians was not a happy one. At least not all the time.

THE CONTEXT FOR PAUL'S LETTERS TO THE CORINTHIANS

The relationship between the founding pastor, Paul, and the believers in Corinth shifted from their barely tolerating Paul to their virulent criticism of him. What Paul wrote, with a pen burning letters onto papyri in our second letter to the Corinthians, gives us more than a glimpse of what the Corinthians, or at least some vocal critics, thought of Paul. In 2 Corinthians 10–13, Paul provides X/Twitter-like (very critical) clips of their criticisms of him. To read one's criticisms of someone else's criticisms of them is not always the easiest way to figure out the criticisms!

Take 2 Corinthians 10:1 as an example. Here Paul writes, "I, Paul, who am 'timid' when face to face with you, but 'bold' toward you when away!" The NIV puts timid and bold in quotations because the translators think Paul is quoting the words of the Corinthians. I agree. These words reveal that they accused Paul of being a milquetoast lightweight people-pleaser when present in Corinth in their house churches. But once he got back to Ephesus, he turned up the harsh tones of his opinions. A second example sounds like the Corinthians thought Paul's physical appearance did not stand up to their idea of a man with such rhetorical and social power: "You are judging by appearances" (10:7). Another indicates they thought he was unpolished and untrained as a public speaker: "his speaking amounts to nothing" (10:10; see 11:5). People-pleasing, unmanly, weak preacher. Not exactly the words you want to read in your inbox when you wake up.

One of the more interesting criticisms concerned Paul's lack of boasting. This one indicates Paul lacked the kind of public bravado and self-confidence they expected of a traveling speaker. "We are not going too far in our boasting . . . neither do we go beyond our limits by boasting of work done by others" (10:14–15). After all, it was Paul's gentile mission that snared the believers in Corinth, but Paul's not taking proper responsibility for his accomplishments. They nail him for it. The flipside of Paul not taking sufficient credit for the wider sweep of his mission was that he was just too humble about it all: "Was it a sin for me to lower myself in order to elevate you by preaching the gospel of God to you free of charge?" (11:7). The people-pleasing, weak preacher lacked social confidence.

That raises the accusation they had with Paul about funding. He evidently did not take funds from them but "robbed," so they say, other churches when he ministered in Corinth (11:8). His principle was not to take funds when planting a church and refusing funds until the church was more self-supporting, and they thought this was a slam on their status. The Corinthians thought they were special, even high-status, a church full of "well knowns" and "who's whos." Paul was not impressed. His choice not to take their money degraded their status in their minds. They went full-on manipulative on this one with a *You-don't-love-us*: "Because I do not love you?" (11:11). They also compared him to those Paul labels as "super-apostles," and he came up short (12:11). This one stung, so Paul pulled out his stinger and said, obliquely but the point is obvious, "persevered in demonstrating among you the marks of a true apostle, including signs, wonders and miracles" (12:12). *So, Corinthians, you think I'm inferior to these megastars. How about considering the miracles done among you?* That's oblique. What he means is *that I did among you*. Bonk! They even accused him of being a "crafty fellow" or using "trickery" (12:16). It is not impossible they thought he did those miracles just mentioned by the powers of sorcerers! Ah, this sounds like accusing Jesus of exorcisms by the power of Satan (Matthew 12:24).

So, the criticisms leveled against him by his own church "parishioners" included:

1. He had a weak, timid personality.
2. He was completely different, that is, he had a strong personality when away.
3. He didn't have the right look.
4. His speaking and preaching skills were lacking.
5. He lacked self-confidence and had many self-hesitations.
6. He degraded their status by not receiving their donations.
7. He didn't love them.
8. He loved other churches more.
9. He wasn't on par with the more prominent Christian leaders.
10. He was tricky and slippery.

Plus, 1 Corinthians contains more of the same (e.g., 4:1–5; 9:1–23). Paul, as pastor and as apostle and as mentor, was anything but warmly received, respected, honored, and praised. He was talked about. He was gossiped about. They degraded him. Divisions are so common in churches. Pastors either put up with a lot or they move on, or in some cases they have good, nice people who mostly leave them alone.

THE SPIRIT AND CIRCLE OF DIVISIVENESS TODAY

The church at Corinth, which means a collection of house churches in Corinth, fell into divisions and factions. Some of their divisions were over Paul. It looks like some preferred Apollos and others Peter. Each faction *knew* it was right, and the others, especially Paul, were wrong. We need to describe that divisiveness, but I will do so with an eye on divisions in churches today. Many churches have suffered from a bout or two (or more) with divisiveness. The spirit of divisiveness remains consistent from group to group. What follows has been aided by more than a half dozen pastors who read the section, commented on it, and gave me feedback. One pastor who read this wrote me a note to say this sketch was prophetic in that it described to a T what occurred in his institution.

TWO NOTS

Briefly, two nots: disagreements over decisions made by leaders *are not* the same as division. Disagreements can become divisive. When discussion with the leader does not accomplish what a person wants to happen, a seed is sown that can lead to division. Learning to tolerate and process differences and disagreements is a mark of a healthy church.

Uniformity from the leader throughout a church *is not* the same as unity. Uniformity is coerced and is top-down; unity is Spirit-prompted and celebrates diversity and difference.

POWER, STATUS, HONOR

First, in Corinth, the heartbeat of the divisive group was the quest for status and honor. It was a zero-sum game driven by a scarcity mindset. That is, *if you got the glory, I didn't.* In our world, that sense of honor comes to expression in the rarely stated desire for *power*, for authority, and for control. The dividers want to be in charge, and they use discord to pave their path to power. When power is understood, as it often is, as authority over and power over, the culture is set for divisiveness to appear. A desire to seize or work for power over a church often flows from a grievance or slight, an act of a leader making a decision the aggrieved didn't like, and a grudge forms that prompts the person to retaliate. One of the watchwords for the divisive is *freedom*, which is as Christian as it is American. The watchword of freedom usually gets an echo in a charge of authoritarianism on the part of those they think ought not to be in power. Behind closed doors the divisive will use terms like "autocrat," "tyrant," and "dictator." The plea by the divisive for freedom is their smokescreen for power. If they do win, as soon as the divisive gain power, they squash the freedom of those whom they fought against. Those who complain the most about unchecked power are those wanting the power for themselves. Nearly all the divisive either diminish their participation or hide from accountability and responsibility for what they have done. Those who set the place on fire and then escape are not deemed heroes for escaping. Division and the power desired by the divisive are fleshly and unspiritual. Virtue and divisiveness cannot hold hands.

7

CLIQUE AND COALITION

Second, disagreement becomes divisive when discussion(s) with the leader or leaders does not lead to what the critic wants. A desire for power begins to build a coalition that turns into a *clique of like-minded disrupters* who go to battle against the leaders. A theme is the old adage: "an enemy of my enemy is a friend." Friends in the tribe like this can be found by dropping little gossips into a conversation to see who might bite. Unlikely but very superficial relations form in these coalitions. People in the church need to become aware of the danger of passive participation in such groups. Not speaking up about the circle of division, when they are noticed, puts a person in the pocket. Hence, a pocket of division, a tribalism, occurs in a church when a disruptive group is formed. Often, such a group creates a sense of chaos, discord, and disunity in the church; the sense that things are out of control. The church leadership will experience division as a struggle for power with others, and the leadership will often need to take action. Disunifiers are shaped by the flesh.

POLITICIZING TENSION POINTS

Third, the *tension points become politicized*. They become zero-sum games. Far too often the tension points are minor issues depicted as major gospel problems. They then become determinative for the divisions. But a wedge can be pressed into service to divide groups over some point. Before long, that point becomes *the* point, regardless of its theological and practical importance. Sides are taken over the tension point. God is with them; God is against the pastor or leader (they want to dismiss). Everything then gets connected to the tension point. He chose—as the leader, as one with the institutional authority to do so, as one who thought he or she had good reasons for the decision—to release a staff member. Disagreement by the circle of division resorts to the language of "tyranny" or "dictatorship," then tyranny becomes the rally cry. Or "heresy" or "false teacher" when the tension point is some truly minor issue in theology or Bible interpretation. What is truly minor and what is major often are confused in the faction of division. Malice and the desire for power drive politicizing these tension points.

LEADER OF THE CLIQUE

Fourth, *someone leads* in nearly all divisions that occur in a church. The person, since he or she wants power, often reveals signs of narcissism. Be warned: it's easy to use the term, but it's a diagnosis that requires a professional. People with narcissistic tendencies are noted by selfishness, a sense of entitlement, a lack of empathy, bold and bald using of others, attracting sycophants, a hypersensitivity to criticism, and especially a desire for personal admiration and glory. When someone over them makes a decision they don't like, the narcissist will diminish the person who made the choice. Remember, the leader of a circle of division wants power. His associates, which at times become nothing less than allegiance, want him or her to have power. Someone, or perhaps a small inner circle, steers the ship of division. Such persons degrade leaders in order to build themselves up. The leader and his inner circle need to be called out for leading the sins of arrogance and division. Opposing the leader of a division is right and good. Some divisive persons love disruption and destruction for no other reason than they love chaos and do not like to be in a system that contains them. The participants in the circle of division usually deny or diminish the very criticisms that describe them.

9

They often then turn the same criticisms onto those who resist their divisiveness.

Words

Fifth, the *primary modes of operation* for the circle of division include gossip about leaders or others, arguing with the leaders, questioning the credentials and ability of the leaders, the desire to attract others in the church to their circle, creating a culture of complaining or sealioning (see For Further Reading on pp. 14), backstabbing and degrading leaders, and labeling the leader with demeaning terms. Labels and names that ridicule often form in the circle of division for those on the outside. Often this circle of division will scapegoat one person or a few persons as the entire problem. Scapegoating, which is very much like canceling, leads to demonizing. None of these verbal habits emerge from the fruit of the Spirit.

End Justifies the Means

Sixth, the circle of division will work together against the leader(s) in order to dismantle authority, degrade the leader(s), and work to get the leader(s) dismissed. Following the procedures matters far less than the desired result of dismissal. For them *the end justifies the means.* When dismissed, the leaders in the circle of division, realizing the depth of their dirty work, often express sadness but internally delight in their victory. Their togetherness strengthens the divisive group's sense of being right. Togetherness does not make division right. Their togetherness means only that they are now a faction of the flesh. Good leaders will need to counter these activities to discover the nature and content of the division, and to counter the fleshly divisions.

THEIR OWN NARRATIVE

Seventh, in working together and thinking they are right, the circle of division *tells itself a story*: it forms its own narrative of the church or institution, claims the high road, refuses to admit their gossip, quotes the Bible for their viewpoints, and contends they are fighting for justice. The circle of division will nearly always tell some truths. Those truths are usually exaggerated or distorted. Only an independent observer, someone marked by wisdom and social perception, can root out the most accurate narrative. Most of the time, the dividers don't even know the deeper, more accurate narrative.

GRANDSTANDING

Eighth, the circle of power, and especially its leader, participate in *grandstanding*, which is a desire to be perceived as virtuous prompted by publicly affirming their own virtues (see Tosi and Warmke, *Grandstanding*). They may host a dinner at one of their homes where they can affirm one another. They may even go to social media. What matters is that they want to be affirmed for the very moral claims they make while bragging about their actions. Here is a definition of grandstanding from the Tosi and Warmke study:

> Grandstanders want to impress others with their moral qualities. We call this the **Recognition Desire**.
> Grandstanders try to satisfy that desire by saying something in public moral discourse. We call this public display the **Grandstanding Expression**.
> You can therefore think of grandstanding in terms of a simple formula:
> **Grandstanding = Recognition Desire + Grandstanding Expression**

Grandstanders try to get others to think of them
as morally respectable. Sometimes they want
to be thought of as one of the gang. Other
times, they want to be thought of as morally
exceptional. Either way, they usually want to be
seen as morally better than others (Tosi, Warmke,
Grandstanding, 15).

When the circle of division, with its strong leaders guiding the circle, doesn't get its way, some leave, some continue to fight until they get what they want, and some learn the lesson that cliques deny the gospel itself.* The first four chapters of 1 Corinthians, not to ignore other passages in Paul's letters, can provide guidance for leaders facing factions in their church or organization.

I have assumed in the above that Paul was more or less on the side of the angels and that his opponents in Corinth were opposing what was good. At times, a pocket forms that is itself the good culture. That pocket of *tov* (or goodness) opposes a toxic leader or leadership. However, how pockets of tov behave in comparison to a circle of division (a pocket of toxicity and power mongering) is completely different, even if resistance and dissidence and disagreements are common to both groups.

THAT COMPLICATED
CORRESPONDENCE WITH CORINTH

A woman named Chloe wrote to Paul with a bundle of questions and some information about how testy the relations were in the church, both between believers and house

---

* I passed this section on divisiveness to half a dozen pastor friends who made comments. I will protect them by not giving their names!

churches and between them and Paul (see 1 Corinthians 1:11–12). At the end of this letter, we learn that three men showed up and filled Paul in on what was happening in Corinth (16:17; Stephanas, Fortunatus, Achaicus).

Paul wrote several letters to Corinth. We have two letters in our New Testament, but many today think especially the second letter combines two or more letters into one. Here's a brief outline of how it all took place, and the following is based on Ralph Martin, *2 Corinthians*, 35–36.

1. Paul founds the church at Corinth AD 49–51 (Acts 18:1–17).
2. Paul departs for Ephesus (Acts 18:18–19).
3. **Letter A**, mentioned in 1 Corinthians 5:9. We don't have this letter. (Is it perhaps behind 2 Corinthians 6:14–7:1?)
4. **Letter B**: Reports about divisions from Chloe's household (1 Corinthians 1:11).
5. Request from some in Corinth by letter for advice (1 Corinthians 7:1).
6. **Letter C**: 1 Corinthians, which responds to Letters A and B and more. Taken to Corinth by Titus, who returns to Paul in Ephesus.
7. Timothy sent to Corinth for pastoral care (1 Corinthians 4:17; 16:10).
8. Crisis in Corinth; someone attacks Paul's leadership (2 Corinthians 2:5–11; 7:8–13). Timothy can't resolve the attack and returns to Ephesus.
9. Paul makes his painful visit to Corinth (2 Corinthians 2:1). Humiliated by their response to him, he returns to Ephesus.
10. **Letter D**: Paul writes the severe letter, which is at least reflected in 2 Corinthians 10–13. Titus requested to meet up with Paul in Troas.

11. Paul goes to Troas; Titus is not there; Paul proceeds to Macedonia (2 Corinthians 2:12–13).
12. Paul learns from Titus that the problem in Corinth is resolved (2 Corinthians 7:6–16).
13. **Letter E**: 2 Corinthians. Titus delivers this letter.
14. More problems in Corinth (2 Corinthians 10:10; 11:27; 12:6–7). Second Corinthians 10–13 may be the response to these problems.
15. Paul arrives in Corinth (Acts 20:2).

Second Corinthians could be a composite of five or six separable letters:

1:1—2:13; 7:5–6
2:14—6:13
6:14—7:1
8 and 9 as two letters, or 8—9 as one letter.
10—13

It's complicated, and in what follows we will avoid this discussion entirely.

FOR FURTHER READING

On sealioning: https://www.merriam-webster.com /words-at-play/sealioning-internet-trolling#
Justin Tosi, Brandon Warmke, *Grandstanding: The Use and Abuse of Moral Talk* (New York: Oxford University Press, 2020).
Ralph Martin, *2 Corinthians*, Second Edition; Word Biblical Commentary: Volume 40 (Grand Rapids: Zondervan, 2014).

DATING PAUL'S LIFE

Early Period: Who's in the Church? (48–57)
    Galatians (48)
        What Are the Problems?:
        1–2 Thessalonians (50)
        1, 2 Corinthians (54, 56)
        Romans (57)

Prison Ministry: What Is the Church? (53–55?)
    Philemon, Colossians, Philippians (c. 53, 54, 55
        or 63?)
    Ephesians (c. 55)

Later Period: What Will the Church Be? (60–62, perhaps 64)
    1–2 Timothy, Titus (c. early 60s)

WORKS CITED IN THE STUDY GUIDE

(Throughout the Guide you will find the author's name and title as noted in this book listing with page numbers whenever I cite something from it):

Charles L. Campbell, *1 Corinthians* (Louisville: Westminster John Knox, 2018). [Campbell, *1 Corinthians*]
Jaime Clark-Soles, *1 Corinthians: Searching the Depths of God* (Nashville: Abingdon, 2021) [Clark-Soles, *1 Corinthians*]

Gordon Fee, *The First Epistle to the Corinthians*, rev. ed. (Grand Rapids: Wm. B. Eerdmans, 2014). [Fee, *First Corinthians*]

Scot McKnight, Lynn H. Cohick, Nijay K. Gupta, *The Dictionary of Paul and His Letters*, revised edition (Downers Grove: IVP Academic, 2023). [*DPL2*]

Scot McKnight, *The Second Testament: A New Translation* (Downers Grove: IVP Academic, 2023) [McKnight, *Second Testament*]

Pheme Perkins, *First Corinthians* (Grand Rapids: Baker Academic, 2012) [Perkins, *First Corinthians*]

Boykin Sanders, "1 Corinthians," in B. Blount, ed., *True to Our Native Land: An African American New Testament Commentary* (Minneapolis: Fortress Press, 2007), 276–306. [Sanders, *1 Corinthians*]

N.T. Wright, Michael Bird, *The New Testament in Its World: An Introduction to the History, Literature, and Theology of the First Christians* (Grand Rapids: Zondervan Academic, 2019). [Wright-Bird, *New Testament World*]

GREETINGS IN CHRIST

1 Corinthians 1:1–9

¹ *Paul, called to be an apostle of Christ Jesus by the will of God, and our brother Sosthenes,*
² *To the church of God in Corinth, to those sanctified in Christ Jesus and called to be his holy people, together with all those everywhere who call on the name of our Lord Jesus Christ—their Lord and ours:*
³ *Grace and peace to you from God our Father and the Lord Jesus Christ.*
⁴ *I always thank my God for you because of his grace given you in Christ Jesus.* ⁵ *For in him you have been enriched in every way—with all kinds of speech and with all knowledge—* ⁶ *God thus confirming our testimony about Christ among you.* ⁷ *Therefore you do not lack any spiritual gift as you eagerly wait for our Lord Jesus Christ to be revealed.* ⁸ *He will also keep you firm to the end, so that you will be blameless on the day of our Lord Jesus Christ.* ⁹ *God is faithful, who has called you into fellowship with his Son, Jesus Christ our Lord.*

I love how Paul starts 1 Corinthians. I love it because every time I read this letter my mind first goes to 2 Corinthians 10–13, which I discussed in the Introduction (pp. 1–16). In that passage, we encounter the nasty things the Corinthians were saying about Paul. That he was weak, that he was not handsome, that his preaching was subpar, that he didn't love them, that he was slimy—and other things, too. Those accusations fill in the background to this letter. Because they do, this opening to the letter is a real shocker. Paul restrains himself, contains himself, says the right things. Instead of launching into an argument, Paul uses the standard format of a letter (writer, addressees, and a thanksgiving). Not only was this format standard, but Paul also touched each part with Christian themes. In short, to open this letter, he goes all pastoral on them. Maybe Paul learned from writing to the Galatians not to come on too angry too quickly.

RESTRAINING YOUR COMMUNICATIONS

Paul may have been tempted to use his own language for what my father called "rummies" or "honyaks." My dad used such terms for the athletes on the high school teams he coached, and they were always used in good fun. I suppose to this day he was at times restraining himself. Paul could have said "What a bunch of losers" or "Grow up, will ya!" Instead, Paul does what he always does with his letters. He begins with the letter writers: "Paul" and he describes himself as "called [by God] to be an apostle of Christ Jesus by the will of God," and then he adds his coauthor, "our brother Sosthenes." Sosthenes appears in Corinth as a local synagogue leader, where he got beat up in front of a major political leader in the city (see Acts 18:17).

Then he mentions to whom he's sending this letter ("church of God in Corinth"), and just to make sure they know how serious he is about who church people really are, he defines it with "to those sanctified in Christ Jesus and called to be his holy people, together with all those everywhere who call on the name of our Lord Jesus Christ—their Lord and ours" (1 Corinthians 1:2). He doubles up with the word "holy," using it behind the translations of both "sanctified" and "holy." A holy person is someone, first of all, dedicated to God—the One who is holy—and, then only second, withdrawn from worldliness, fleshiness, and sinfulness. He triples with the word "call" in our passage: "called to be an apostle" and "called to be his holy people" and "call on the name of our Lord Jesus." Two of these are God's calling on humans and one a human calling on the Lord. Christians are called by their calling. The third element of his greeting blesses the Corinthians with "grace and peace" (1:3).

THANKING GOD FOR THE PEOPLE

Verses four through nine are one long and winding sentence. In which long sentence Paul restrains himself especially by informing them of a continual practice on his part: giving thanks "always" for them (Weima, "Prayer"). His three-times-a-day prayers, which he learned as a child, meant praying for the Corinthians at least three times each day. Gordon Fee, a premier scholar of Paul and this letter, writes "what is remarkable here is the apostle's ability to thank God for the very things in this church that, because of the abuses, are also causing him grief" (Fee, *First Corinthians*, 33). His thanksgiving is directed at the faithful God who hangs on to believers (1:4, 8, 9) because this God has empowered them with the kind of "grace" that comes to fruition in the spiritual gifts of "speech" and "knowledge," which nods toward chapters twelve through fourteen where these two sorts of gifts had become problematic.

Paul knows these Corinthians "do not lack any spiritual gift" (1:7). They may be on a bit of a status trip of Who's Who in the Roman way of determining honor, but they are also filled with the gifts of the Spirit. People with lots of talent who also have spiritual giftedness can be hard to handle. Paul was deeply familiar with the problem. Paul places the believers in Corinth onto a timeline: they were pagans, they turned to Jesus, and now they "early await" for the Lord Jesus to be "revealed" at the end of the age (1:7). That end will usher all creation to the kingdom of God. Finally, Paul lays out their calling as they wait: "fellowship with his Son, Jesus Christ our Lord" (1:9). They share their life in common (the meaning of "fellowship") with Jesus. Which means their calling is, to adapt the famous expression of Brother Lawrence, "to practice the presence of Jesus." To live in constant communication with Jesus—from sunup to sundown, and when we awake in the dark hours of the night.

GOD OVER ALL

Paul shuts the door on the opening to the letter by turning to God. Paul knows God's over all, that the church in Corinth is not his but God's, and that he has been called by God. This "God is faithful." Not only is God faithful, but this God has "called" these very divided Corinthians to live a common life, all day long every day, in the presence of Jesus Christ. Even if they are divided, and even if Paul's irritated into rashes over them, they are God's and God's calling on them is no different than God's general calling on them. In the middle of chapter three, Paul will write "you are God's field, God's building" and "God's temple" and by that he means *not mine, not Apollos's, and not Cephas's* (3:9, 16 and 1:12). Restraint can be sustained by turning to God.

A Time to . . .

It's hard to restrain yourself when you are in strained relations with others. At times restraint feels fake and hypocritical. It's even harder to restrain yourself when you know people around you are fomenting divisions. Perhaps Paul's positive approach in opening the letter resulted from the lesson that there's a time to sting and a time to sing. To open this letter, Paul chose the latter. The sting was not far off.

Questions for Reflection and Application

1. How does Paul's letter opening work to remind the people of Corinth who they are (or at least, who they are supposed to be)?

2. How might Paul's thanksgiving and prayer for these people help him relate to them in the face of their unkindness to him?

3. What can you learn about good pastoral communication from the start of this letter?

4. What have you learned about restraining your communications through your experiences of conflict?

5. Reflecting on the opening section of this Bible study guide, what do you think about the proposed difference between uniformity and unity?

FOR FURTHER READING

Brother Lawrence, *Practicing the Presence of God* (Washington, D.C.: ICS Publications, 2015). J.A.D. Weima, "Prayer," in *DPL 2*: 838–845, esp. 838–839.

CLIQUES AND
THE CROSS

1 Corinthians 1:10–17

[10] I appeal to you, brothers and sisters, in the name of our Lord Jesus Christ, that all of you agree with one another in what you say and that there be no divisions among you, but that you be perfectly united in mind and thought. [11] My brothers and sisters, some from Chloe's household have informed me that there are quarrels among you. [12] What I mean is this: One of you says, "I follow Paul"; another, "I follow Apollos"; another, "I follow Cephas"; still another, "I follow Christ."

[13] Is Christ divided? Was Paul crucified for you? Were you baptized in the name of Paul? [14] I thank God that I did not baptize any of you except Crispus and Gaius, [15] so no one can say that you were baptized in my name. [16] (Yes, I also baptized the household of Stephanas; beyond that, I don't remember if I baptized anyone else.) [17] For Christ did not send me to baptize, but to preach the gospel—not with wisdom and eloquence, lest the cross of Christ be emptied of its power.

One theme pervades this entire letter: living together in a church divided. The tensions are real, the divisions are clear, and the desire of the apostle Paul continues to be heard. He hopes and strives for living together well, for unity, and for community. "Community," Jaime Clark-Soles writes in her wonderful little book about this letter of Paul's, "is simultaneously crucial and complicated" (Clark-Soles, *1 Corinthians*, xvi). Some pages later she lays out the solution for Paul: "Paul models cooperation instead of competition" (Clark-Soles, *1 Corinthians*, 11). We need both of her sound observations because church life is bound to get messy. Complicated. Competitive.

This complication at times unravels into cliques. The divisive can do no other: they must gather into cliques in their pursuit of power. They find those who will connect with their criticisms and their (supposedly better) ideas. And they express allegiance to a name, to a person, to a charismatic personality, to someone with talent, authority, and smarts. In their clique, they have power and a feeling that they are the ones in the right. Not cooperation. Paul addresses the problem with cliques in Corinth in today's passage, and his instructions are clear and direct. A few of his terms summarize for us his instructions about cliques, and then we turn to what to do about the divisions if we want to form community. He gets his information about the cliques from some from Chloe's household (1:11). Paul knows he has to call out the factions in Corinth, not so he can enter into the factionalism, but so he can end the divisions.

CLIQUES

The sting can now be felt. Paul accuses the Corinthians of forming cliques, tribes sealed off from others. What unites each tribe is not some special theology but the opportunity to gain power for what they think needs to happen for the house churches in Corinth. Paul urges them to have no "divisions," or rips in the fellowship. Another aspect of their

cliques is that there are "quarrels" (1:10, 11). The word translated "quarrels" is from the Greek word *eris*, which in Paul's
world frequently referred to the effects of social-climbing
and status-seeking and money-flashing. It is the kind of
quarrel that occurs in rivalries rather than simply the arguments of intellectuals. The word describes those who think
the leader (Paul) is wrong and that their particular angle is
right. If the churches don't side with them, the whole place
will collapse. People can disagree in a fellowship, but cliques
form when disagreement morphs into a desire for power (see
Beaty, *Celebrities for Jesus*). Paul desires, according to a fresh
translation of verse ten, that "they be restored" back to the
same mind (Sanders, *1 Corinthians*, 280–281; NIV has "perfectly united"). Paul knows their past, and in this case wants
them to get back where they were in their former unity.

Apollos in 1 Corinthians

What I mean is this: One of you says, "I follow
Paul"; another, "I follow Apollos"; another, "I follow
Cephas"; still another, "I follow Christ." (1:12)

For when one says, "I follow Paul," and another, "I follow Apollos," are you not mere human beings? What,
after all, is Apollos? And what is Paul? Only servants,
through whom you came to believe—as the Lord has
assigned to each his task. I planted the seed, Apollos
watered it, but God has been making it grow (3:4–6).

. . . whether Paul or Apollos or Cephas or the world
or life or death or the present or the future—all are
yours (3:22).

Now, brothers and sisters, I have applied these things to myself and Apollos for your benefit, so that you may learn from us the meaning of the saying, "Do not go beyond what is written." Then you will not be puffed up in being a follower of one of us over against the other (4:6).

Now about our brother Apollos: I strongly urged him to go to you with the brothers. He was quite unwilling to go now, but he will go when he has the opportunity (16:12).

Cliques form around names connected to authority and (potential) power (see Introduction, pp. 1–16). Cliquish people seek for authorities who will support them. Paul names the names in Corinth, and they are early Christian leaders: Paul himself, Apollos, Cephas, and Christ. The first are those who are more or less allegiant to Paul's gospel and are fighting off others. The second connects to the rhetorician himself, Apollos, and the appeal of a public speaker is well-known for the Corinthians. The cliques may have centered on him. The third name's an apostle who made a passing visit to Corinth, Cephas, the Aramaic name for Peter (9:5). To claim "Christ" makes one suspect some were saying "Let's get back to Jesus" in a superficial way. Paul himself will anchor his vision to end the cliques in God's work in Christ and the Spirit. It is not impossible that Peter's got a group of followers in Corinth. It is more than possible for Apollos. It is possible that the named leaders are the imagined leaders by the members of these cliques. But as we will discover in 3:1–4, the clique opposed to Paul in Corinth favored Apollos, with his famous rhetorical skills.

The evangelical church throughout the world is profoundly cliquish. Evangelicals seem to have a yearning desire for a hero to prop themselves up with someone with status and power or money. A friend of mine once did a study of America's churches, and one of his discoveries was that churches are increasingly no longer loyal to a denomination. Their allegiance is to one of America's megachurch pastors and his theories and strategies. Some pastors thus pass the scent test of the cliques of Corinth. Their branding of their church and their theology seem to form cliques and their lack of cooperation with others, unless totally on board with their branding, supports the suspicion. Not competition but cooperation, remember. Living together means stopping the competition.

FALSE ALLEGIANCES

Paul calls them to attention with questions that have (assumed) answers. (1) "Is Christ split into parts"? (McKnight, *Second Testament*). No. (2) "Was Paul crucified for you?" No. (3) "Or were you dipped into the name of Paulos?" (McKnight, *Second Testament*). No. *If the answers are no, the cliques are flat-out wrong-headed.* Christ forms a united body; Christ was the one crucified and who brings forgiveness. Christ is the one in whose name they were baptized. It's all about Jesus. Their claims to power and authority in the names of Paul, Apollos, Cephas, and the false claim to Christ, proves they now have false allegiances.

"Cult followings," or in nicer moments, "cult-like followings," is what we call it today. The reality is that we all want good leaders who have good character and who nurture Christlikeness. We will honor those who do. Paul will twice in this letter instruct the Corinthians to follow or imitate or copy him (4:16–17; 11:1). Valuing one's spiritual mentor is good. Some mentors arrogantly press people into a level of devotion and allegiance that turns into spiritual codependency. Such spiritual codependency turns into an allegiance to a human. Such false allegiances are usually unconscious. But the mentor becomes the mediator between that person and God, and that person looks to that mentor for approval instead of to God. The allegiance becomes fandom, devotion, and ultimately idolatry. Paul will, if I can use the expression, punch this kind of allegiance, and the leader(s) of the clique, in the nose in this letter and in 2 Corinthians, too.

Cult-like allegiances are addictions at the emotional, psychological, and spiritual levels. The addicted cannot not be allegiant; the addiction is invisible; the addiction is rationalized and even spiritualized. Addictive allegiances in cliques are hard habits to break, but they must be because false allegiances are idolatrous. Often, it requires an outsider to point out the false allegiance. Very few catch the pointing-out the first time. They may deny the addiction altogether. Firm words, as we see in Paul, are needed. We hope they are anointed with prayer and the power of the Spirit. Jaime Clark-Soles is right: it's complicated.

WHAT TO DO?

Paul gets right to the point and begins with a claim to his apostolic authority: "I appeal to you . . . in the name of our Lord Jesus Christ" (1:10). First, they are to "say the same thing," a Greek way of saying "agree with one another" (1:10). Second, he flat out prohibits cliquishness: "I appeal to you . . . that there be no divisions" (1:10). Cliques are wrong. Allegiances to power-seekers and status-seekers counter the gospel itself. They deny the unity that is in Christ; they split what Christ accomplished on the cross; they disconnect from one's baptism in the name of Christ. Practically, cliques often fail to recognize human realities that deny the false allegiances. Paul didn't even baptize these people, and some are claiming him as their authority. The human reality is that Paul has been called, not to "wisdom and eloquence," but to "preach the gospel" about Jesus Christ. Where he focuses in the gospel is on the "cross of Christ." Why? Because it reveals humility, the human need for grace, and the lack of worldly wisdom and power (1:13–17).

The solution to the cliques of Corinth is the cross of Christ.

QUESTIONS FOR REFLECTION AND APPLICATION

1. What is Paul's strategic approach to addressing the divisions in Corinth?

2. How did the secular cultural values of status-seeking lead to the quarrels among the Christian community?

3. How does competition in a church body hinder cooperation?

4. How have you seen cult-like allegiances to particular leaders form cliques in churches?

5. What do you think are some differences between a healthy spiritual mentor and a mentor who demands fan-like levels of devotion?

FOR FURTHER READING

Katelyn Beaty, *Celebrities for Jesus: How Personas, Platforms, and Profits Are Hurting the Church* (Grand Rapids: Brazos Press, 2022).

STATUS CLAIMS
AND THE CROSS

1 Corinthians 1:18–2:5

[18] *For the message of the cross is foolishness to those who are perishing, but to us who are being saved it is the power of God.* [19] *For it is written:*

> *"I will destroy the wisdom of the wise;*
> *the intelligence of the intelligent I will frustrate."*

[20] *Where is the wise person? Where is the teacher of the law? Where is the philosopher of this age? Has not God made foolish the wisdom of the world?* [21] *For since in the wisdom of God the world through its wisdom did not know him, God was pleased through the foolishness of what was preached to save those who believe.* [22] *Jews demand signs and Greeks look for wisdom,* [23] *but we preach Christ crucified: a stumbling block to Jews and foolishness to Gentiles,* [24] *but to those whom God has called, both Jews and Greeks, Christ the power of God and the wisdom of God.* [25] *For the foolishness of God is wiser than human wisdom, and the weakness of God is stronger than human strength.*

[26] *Brothers and sisters, think of what you were when you were called. Not many of you were wise by human standards; not many*

were influential; not many were of noble birth. [27] But God chose the foolish things of the world to shame the wise; God chose the weak things of the world to shame the strong. [28] God chose the lowly things of this world and the despised things—and the things that are not— to nullify the things that are, [29] so that no one may boast before him. [30] It is because of him that you are in Christ Jesus, who has become for us wisdom from God—that is, our righteousness, holiness and redemption. [31] Therefore, as it is written: "Let the one who boasts boast in the Lord."

[2:1] And so it was with me, brothers and sisters. When I came to you, I did not come with eloquence or human wisdom as I proclaimed to you the testimony about God. [2] For I resolved to know nothing while I was with you except Jesus Christ and him crucified. [3] I came to you in weakness with great fear and trembling. [4] My message and my preaching were not with wise and persuasive words, but with a demonstration of the Spirit's power, [5] so that your faith might not rest on human wisdom, but on God's power.

The word on the streets of Corinth could have been expressed with the Latin word *Romanitas*: the desire to look like, act like, and be given status and honor like a Roman. Corinth was filled with Rome wannabes. Achieving Rome's status symbols gave people in Corinth honor (Winter, *After Paul Left*, 1–28). In our day, status can be marked by driving a Porsche into the church parking lot. Or by telling a gaggle of folks that you have just returned from Italy, not just any place in Italy, but from Portofino. Or by using a foreign word, like *Romanitas*, that could give off a whiff of sophistication. Or by reminding someone in the office, with a touch of indirection, that you have the power to hire and fire. Or that your church has lots of deep pockets and big givers, and that they expect you, their pastor, to attend events with high society. Or that you are a member of the local posh country club. Or that your "kicks" cost $$$$. I could go on. You know the drill. We will never be totally redeemed from our desire to be noticed (or more).

The house churches of Corinth had their own jet set, and their own poor and enslaved persons. It was a multi-status church. Erastus was the director of public works (Romans 16:23), Crispus was a synagogue leader (1 Corinthians 1:14; Acts 18:8), we know names of some heads of households (like Stephanas and Chloe; cf. 1 Corinthians 1:11, 14, 16; 11:22; 16:15), some others had sufficient funds to support Paul with connections and resources and funds (like Gaius, Titus Justus, Phoebe; 1 Corinthians 1:14; Acts 18:17; Romans 16:1–2), and we know Aquila and Priscilla were sufficiently funded to travel and work in various places, but they needed to work as artisans to provide for themselves (1 Corinthians 16:19; Romans 16:3). Not to be ignored would be the lower classes, the poor, and slaves (1 Corinthians 7:21; 12:13; 11:22; Wright-Bird, *New Testament World*, 482). A Roman society graded humans on the basis of a person's heritage, military accomplishments, public benevolence, and even public speaking. Privilege ruled Roman society. At the top was the emperor with citizenry split into two major permanent groups: patricians (people with heritage and wealth) and plebians (the rest of the citizens, who were patronized by the patricians). The government class of Rome and Roman societies was composed of senators (most were patricians) or equestrians (knights).

In Corinth, the pursuit of glory and status, the wisdom of this world, conflicted with a life shaped by the cross, the wisdom of God. Gordon Fee calls the conflict between the human quest for honor and the cross the "ultimate divine contradiction" (Fee, *First Corinthians*, 78). Today's passage displays this conflict, so we will take one theme at a time. If you like to mark your Bible, you could mark in a different color which expressions indicate worldly wisdom and which have God's wisdom. By the way, our passage begins a section that extends all the way to 3:23. Living together well will require us to take a fearless look at what's actually going on in our churches.

WISDOM OF THE WORLD

The clash of cosmic realities in Corinth occurred at both the level of ideas and practices. By practices, I mean the way people behaved and related with one another. High-status folks had the habit of keeping low-status folks in their place, which meant keeping themselves in their place. Much could be said about this, but people of privilege maintain their privilege in many ways, not least in policies, laws, practices—intentional or not, conscious or not—that maintain privilege at the expense of excluding others from that privilege. We use the word "welfare" for what poor people are given by the government. But more government money is distributed in cash and benefits and resources to the wealthy than to the poor. "If you count all public benefits offered by the federal government, America's welfare state (as a share of its gross domestic product) is the second biggest in the world, after France's. But that's true only if you include things like government-subsidized retirement benefits provided by employers, student loans and 529 college savings plans, child tax credits, and homeowner subsidies: benefits disproportionately flowing to Americans well above the poverty line. If you put aside these tax breaks and judge the United States solely by the share of its GDP allocated to programs directed at low-income citizens, our investment in poverty reduction is much smaller than that of other rich nations. The American welfare state is lopsided" (Desmond, *Poverty, By America*, 91). That we use the term "welfare" only for the poor reveals that it belongs to "them" and not to "us," but we are the beneficiaries.

34

Notice how Paul describes their and our sort of wisdom of the world in today's passage, and I don't provide references to keep from clogging up the sentences. He calls it "foolishness" and the "wisdom of the world" and "human wisdom" and "human strength" and "human standards" and "signs" and "influential" (or social power) and "noble birth" and the "wise" and the "strong" and "eloquence" and "wise and persuasive words." Three times the NIV has "human wisdom," which can be the summary expression for Paul.

There are a few expressions here that open the door for us to enter and observe what was happening in the house churches. I imagine this on the basis of these terms: some people had a noble heritage, that is, they had status in the Roman system. Perhaps equestrians. Perhaps even patricians but more likely plebians with some real estate, wealth, and social power. Their social power flowed from their "human wisdom," which was based on "human standards," and they had "human [social] strength" because of their "noble birth" and their "eloquence." These were well-spoken, intelligent, socially gifted, and socially known believers in the church of Corinth.

The social positions of some of these Corinthians are found in these terms: "wise person" and "teacher of the law [of Moses]" and "philosopher of this age," or "this Era's disputer" (McKnight, *Second Testament*). Those in Paul's mind who are troubling the churches in Corinth are those with social standing and verbal skills. They are the ones standing up front, leading the room, and guiding the board. Not many of that sort were believers. But their power and authority in the Corinthian assemblies transcended their numbers. Notice Paul's repeated words: "Not many . . . not many . . . not many of you" (1:26). Paul inserted a few lines back a very serious warning about the Corinthian way of life. It marks those who are "perishing" not those who "are being saved"

(1:18). They are marked by the behaviors that characterize "this age." The cross sits in judgment on all this. The cross measures the wisdom of God. Over and over in today's passage you will read that this world has been shocked by the act of God, the revelation of Jesus Christ on the cross. Every script in the Roman way gets flipped by the script of the cross. "Not many of you . . ." remember, is how Paul puts it.

An analogy will bring this to clarity with ease: on most church boards you will find white men who are socially skilled businessmen or corporate types, lawyers, medical experts and scientists, and those with social power in the community. At times, and in some cases more often than that, they are on boards because of their human [social] status and power, not because of their spiritual maturity, theological expertise, or pastoral gifts. That's Corinth all over again. When Corinth types sit behind closed doors making decisions for the whole church on the basis of their skill set in the corporate or law or science world, they have some chance of getting things mostly right. But often, their judgments are skewed because they are insufficiently shaped by the wisdom of God.

WISDOM OF GOD

In contrast with *Romanitas*'s quest for social honor, instead of signs and wisdom, instead of power and social influence, Paul shoves forward nothing less than his most controversial vision for how followers of Jesus are to conduct themselves in Corinth. His watchword over and over and over and over: "cross of Christ" (1:17). A second century Roman leader, Pliny, called the cross-shaped vision of Christians "nothing but a debased superstition carried to great lengths" (Pliny, *Epistles* 10.96.8). The logic of the cross leads to both humility (before God and with one another) as well as unity with one another. Paul himself was a witness for this approach to living the logic of the cross, what Michael Gorman has called over and over "cruciformity" and which I like to call "Christoformity." Paul, in one sense, bragged that he himself could be persuaded and could persuade others on the basis of what he had accomplished by human, Jewish standards (Philippians 3:5–6). Instead of that sort of persuasion, Paul chose to forfeit what he had accomplished for the sake of Christ. He even considers his accomplishments as "feces" (3:7–11; *Second Testament*).

In our passage, the ideas at work in his watchword include "message of the cross" as the "power of God," whether it climbs up to social power or not! And the "wisdom of God" and "the foolishness of what was preached" and "Christ crucified" are three pregnant expressions for Paul. God has "called" all believers to this gospel and a life that looks like "Christ crucified." This message is, looking at it through the lens of *Romanitas*, the "foolishness of God" and the "weakness of God" and, notice this, is what the "testimony about God" sounds like. Living and preaching this gospel operates with the "Spirit's power" and "God's power."

A word about preaching. Paul's statement that he did not come to Corinth with the skills gained through education of "eloquence and human wisdom" (2:1). Some think Paul does not believe in the skills of communication, but no one can read Paul's letters, not least Romans, and not be impressed with his abilities. Rather, what Paul's against is the self-promotion, the pride, and the pursuit of glory that can be acquired by the one on the platform behind the pulpit (McKnight, *Pastor Paul*, 159–161).

CORINTH IN OUR DAY

One might ask how we can do this in our churches. It's too easy to point long fingers with snarled noses at the Corinthians and to ignore our own similar ways of life. How can we avoid *Romanitas* in order to communicate with clarity the gospel about Christ crucified, the message of the cross? The first thing is to get out of the way. You and I need to see ourselves as mediators and agents of God's message about Jesus Christ instead of people who are gaining status and power and celebrity. The second thing is to find friends who can observe us and listen to us and offer the wisdom of the cross as the mirror in which we see ourselves. If we reject them, or worse, turn to retaliation, we have exposed ourselves as those addicted to *Romanitas*, whether we see it and confess it ourselves or not. If when we are told the truth, we have to rip the sutures tying together our lips and then to defend ourselves, with vehemence, we need to read this passage all over again. We need more "Christ crucified" and less "influential" and "human standards" and "noble birth."

A counter point in ministry. Some people degrade themselves, see themselves as imposters, feel shame over their body or gender or accomplishments or lack of status (even when they have it). Some were ignored or fell into the cracks of their family: loved *and* ignored often results in the feeling of unworthiness. For such persons, Paul's cracking the whip about *Romanitas* will feel wounding, and can lead to a deeper spin into the vortex of shame. Paul's words are not for them. His words for them are the comforting words that we are elevated with a gospel social power and status because in Christ we know a "wisdom from God" and that Jesus is "our righteousness, holiness and redemption" and that we can "boast in the Lord" (1:30–31).

A distinction between two words may help all of us. The two words are "jealousy" and "envy." The second word points at us when we want what others have—a bigger home, a fancier car, a better job, a network with so-and-so in it, an affluent income, a higher position on the flow chart. Envy is to want what others have and drives the American spirit of competition (instead of cooperation). Jealousy, though used all the time for envy, points at a person's status and their efforts to gain it, to sustain it, and to protect it. When a person moves into your faith community with skills better than yours in leadership, speaking, and influence, you may experience jealousy over the status you formerly had. Both envy and jealousy are *Romanitas*, especially the latter.

QUESTIONS FOR REFLECTION AND APPLICATION

1. What similarities and differences do you see between the ways status was displayed and measured in the Roman Empire and today?

2. Why did the cross of Christ look like foolishness to people seeking *Romanitas*?

3. What do you think of the revelation that the USA's government subsidies go more to the already rich than to the poor?

4. Do you feel the sting of Paul's words correcting your own status-seeking, or do you feel his grace for people marginalized by society who carry the wisdom of God?

5. In what ways have you seen church leadership positions given to people with worldly wisdom and status instead of godly wisdom?

FOR FURTHER READING

Matthew Desmond, *Poverty, By America* (New York: Crown, 2023).

Michael Gorman, *Cruciformity*, new edition (Grand Rapids: Wm. B. Eerdmans, 2020).

Scot McKnight, *Pastor Paul* (Grand Rapids: Brazos, 2019).

Pliny, *Epistles* https://www.attalus.org/old/pliny10b.html (trans. J.B. Firth with minor revisions).

Bruce Winter, *After Paul Left Corinth* (Grand Rapids: Wm. B. Eerdmans, 2001).

SPIRIT-WISDOM
IN THE CROSS

1 Corinthians 2:6–16

6 We do, however, speak a message of wisdom among the mature, but not the wisdom of this age or of the rulers of this age, who are coming to nothing. 7 No, we declare God's wisdom, a mystery that has been hidden and that God destined for our glory before time began. 8 None of the rulers of this age understood it, for if they had, they would not have crucified the Lord of glory.

9 However, as it is written:

> *"What no eye has seen,*
> > *what no ear has heard,*
> *and what no human mind has conceived"—*
> > *the things God has prepared for those who*
> > > *love him—*

10 these are the things God has revealed to us by his Spirit.
The Spirit searches all things, even the deep things of God. 11 For who knows a person's thoughts except their own spirit within them? In the same way no one knows the thoughts of God except the Spirit of God. 12 What we have received is not the spirit of the world, but the Spirit who is from God, so that we may understand what God

has freely given us. [13] This is what we speak, not in words taught us by human wisdom but in words taught by the Spirit, explaining spiritual realities with Spirit-taught words. [14] The person without the Spirit does not accept the things that come from the Spirit of God but considers them foolishness, and cannot understand them because they are discerned only through the Spirit. [15] The person with the Spirit makes judgments about all things, but such a person is not subject to merely human judgments, [16] for,

> *"Who has known the mind of the Lord*
> *so as to instruct him?"*

But we have the mind of Christ.

The apostle Paul was known, and still is, for his claims to know what others did not know. He probably got under the skin of plenty of his contemporaries. He still irritates his readers. Today's passage is filled with those "irritating" claims by Paul. Paul turns from a bleak depiction of the fleshly, worldly-wisdom-based, status-driven origins of divisions among the house churches in Corinth to a depiction of the world of God's wisdom, which has been given to the believers through the Spirit. The one group is "mature" (2:6) and the toxic, divisive group is a nursery of "infants" (3:1). One group is adulting, the other is not. As my daughter and I had to describe toxic cultures in order to describe *tov* (good) cultures, Paul all over again had to dip into the toxicities at work in Corinth, describing their way of life as "the wisdom of this age," before he could get to genuine Spirit-prompted wisdom (McKnight, Barringer, *A Church Called Tov*). Only this Spirit-prompted wisdom could lead them to living together as God designs.

In our passage Paul takes a favorite term of the divisive group in Corinth, the term "wisdom," criticizes it and then picks up the term for himself and redefines it by the cross of Christ. If you ask Paul, *What's wisdom?*, he would hold up for you a wooden cross. Every verse in today's passage irritated the divisive in Corinth because of his claims to know what they did not know. I suspect over coffee Paul may have muttered matter-of-factly, *If you know, you know.* If he's right, he did know. Irritating or not.

This Age's Wisdom

Calvin Miller, one of a former generation's most accomplished pastors and writers, said,

> Some of the "big" pastors I know seem to enjoy being "big." They own a sense of success and fame that satisfies most of them. And they are revered generally for being deeply spiritual men, even loving men. But the best of pastors realize that good sermons are not just flashy rhetoric. Sermons are only noble when they are so "see-through" that the pastor's need for God is clearly visible through his words. (Miller, *Life Is Mostly Edges*, 228)

What Miller means with "big" is what Paul means with the wisdom of "this age." The word Paul uses is *aionios*, which means an era or an age or a period of time. The twentieth century was an *aionios* as also was the *ainiois* of the northern kingdom. I lived through the *aionios* of the manual typewriter, of the electric typewriter, and of the computer. We are now in an *aionios* of hybrid workplaces.

For Paul, "this age" is the present world ruled by Satan, sin, sickness, and systemic evil. Not to ignore the emperor and other government authorities, and perhaps the principalities and powers ("rulers of this age"; 2:6). With the identical expression, Paul called believers out of the present *aionios* when he wrote in Romans 12:2, "Do not conform to the pattern of this *aionios*" (the NIV translates with "world"). This age and its rulers, Paul predicts, "are coming to nothing" (1 Corinthians 2:6). None of them comprehend the mystery of God's wisdom revealed in Jesus Christ. That they crucified Jesus reveals their blindness (2:8). Stand back to notice that Paul depicts life on this earth as an era prior to the eternal kingdom of God, and believers are to live now as if the kingdom were here!

Spirit-Prompted Wisdom

This-world-based, elitist wisdom, these claims to special wisdom, discerned only by the human mind and calculation and intuition and speculation and committee work, contrasts with "God's wisdom" and the "mystery." And especially with Spirit-prompted wisdom, which is the heartbeat of today's passage. Spirit-ual wisdom becomes the topic from verse nine through sixteen. I don't like those "there are two kinds of people" sayings, except when I do! There are two kinds of Christians: those who speak about the Spirit too much, and those who speak about the Spirit not often enough. Paul stands on two solid feet to gain the balance of when to and when not to talk Spirit-talk. Today's passage is one of his most famous *Yes, let's talk about the Spirit* passages.

God's wisdom was for Paul a fresh apocalypse by God. He quotes something that sounds like or paraphrases Isaiah 64:4.* Then Paul says no one had seen, heard, experienced, or

---

* Isaiah 64:4 in the NIV reads, "From ages past no one has heard, no ear has perceived, no eye has seen any God besides you, who works for those who wait for him." It may echo Isaiah 65:17 as well: "See, I will create new heavens and a new earth. The former things will not be remembered, nor will they come to mind."

even imagined the goodness of God's revelation designed for "those who love him" (1 Corinthians 2:9). The content and experience of this apocalypse is "revealed to us by his Spirit" (2:10). Paul claims believers in Jesus Christ *know and experience a reality unknowable and unexperienced by unbelievers.* Only those indwelt by God's revealing Spirit know this wisdom. He repeats this in other words a few verses later with "the person without the Spirit does not accept" the Spirit's revelations. (Behind this translation by the NIV, more literally, is "a selfish human" [*psychikos anthrōpos*, a self-based, psychical person]). Such a person, echoing those of 1:18–25, considers such wisdom "foolishness" but only because only those with the Spirit comprehend gospel truths.

The Spirit knows God, the Father and the Son (2:11). The Spirit's mission from Father and Son includes the redemptive regeneration of the mind and heart to know the truth of God's wisdom. A Spirit-indwelt person "examines all things" and, because such a person has been lifted into the Spirit's truth, cannot be "examined" by a person anchored in the wisdom of this age (2:15; *Second Testament*). How could they? They know not the Spirit. Paul connects the Spirit's revelations of wisdom to believers with the "mind of the Lord," which echoes 2:11—the Spirit knows the Father and the Son. Knowing is one thing, speaking is another. Paul's evangelistic and teaching missions involve speaking "words taught by the Spirit, explaining spiritual realities with Spirit-taught words" (2:13). One must stand back to see the stunning claim Paul puts on paper. Paul claims that believers in Jesus Christ have passed from this age into the next age, from human to divine wisdom. Philosophers rightly see here Paul making a claim at the level of epistemology, the science of knowing. The words of C.S. Lewis for many of us have expressed the Christian claim the best: "I believe in Christianity as I believe that the sun has risen: not only because I see it, but because by it I see everything else" (C.S. Lewis, "They Asked for a Paper," 164–165).

Spirit-prompted wisdom unifies believers; the wisdom of this age, *Romanitas*, divides. Paul accuses the partisans in Corinth of using their worldly wisdom and appeals to them to surrender the unifying wisdom that alone comes to them through the Spirit. Spirit-based wisdom comprehends all of reality through the humility of Christ-crucified, through the revelation that comes from God and not from status-seeking.

The claims just made are dangerous in the hands of some, and I wish to close our section with this: we should not make too much of what we know. It is not like we *know facts* otherwise unknowable. Once we know those facts, and once we make them known, others can *understand* those facts. What we do "know" then is *the location of those facts in a larger, meaning-making story or metanarrative*. It's the story that God has revealed himself in Jesus Christ—his life, his teachings, his actions, his death, his burial, his resurrection, his ascension, his return—and because we see the truth of the gospel in Jesus, we see all things *through that gospel*. That gospel story is God's wisdom. It is not understandable to others because others have chosen to understand reality and the same facts through another story. Which is why Paul caps off today's passage as he does: "But we have the mind of Christ" (2:16). A mind shaped by the Christ-story is a new mind, a mind only those who believe in Christ care to appropriate.

QUESTIONS FOR REFLECTION
AND APPLICATION

1. How does Paul broadly redefine "wisdom"?

2. What does "this age" mean to Paul, and what does it have to do with this wisdom discussion?

3. What are the differences between human wisdom and Spirit wisdom?

4. How does the gospel lead to wisdom?

5. How could you gain more Spirit-wisdom in your life?

FOR FURTHER READING

C.S. Lewis, *Is Theology Poetry?* (reprint from a lecture 1944; Samizdat: University Press, 2014), 15. See at: http://www.samizdat.qc.ca/arts/lit /Theology=Poetry_CSL.pdf.

Scot McKnight and Laura Barringer, *A Church Called Tov* (Carol Stream: Tyndale Momentum, 2020).

Calvin Miller, *Life Is Mostly Edges: A Memoir* (Nashville: Thomas Nelson, 2008).

CLIQUE AND
THE CROSS

1 Corinthians 3:1–4

[1] *Brothers and sisters, I could not address you as people who live by the Spirit but as people who are still worldly—mere infants in Christ.* [2] *I gave you milk, not solid food, for you were not yet ready for it. Indeed, you are still not ready.* [3] *You are still worldly. For since there is jealousy and quarreling among you, are you not worldly? Are you not acting like mere humans?* [4] *For when one says, "I follow Paul," and another, "I follow Apollos," are you not mere human beings?*

Speaking, as we did in the last passage, of irritation, Paul is irritated about the divisions in Corinth. He probably wanted to kick 'em in their keisters. Today's passage shows he has not at all dropped his concern about these rips in the fellowship. And did you notice the absence of Cephas and even of the so-called Christ party in verse four? The parties are reduced to two: Paul and Apollos. Many of us think the opponents of Paul in Corinth were followers of Apollos. Notice also 3:5 and 4:6. Or they thought they were. It is not at all clear that Apollos sided with them.

So, we're back to the divisive people and their *Romanitas*. I define what divisive people are all about: First, the germ of divisiveness sprouts into a desire for *power*, for authority, and for control. Second, disagreements are common. They become divisive when the desire for power turns into a *clique of like-minded disrupters* who go to battle against the leaders. The circle of division occurs in a church when a disruptive group is formed. Their power mongering turns into a power struggle, they are usually led by someone who wants to be the authority, and their mode of operation always is verbal attack, innuendo, gossip, slander, and libel. They want to be not just on the platform, but be the platform itself (Beaty, *Celebrities for Jesus*).

Paul is irritated, and his language shows it. If he is right in discerning them as divisive, and if he is right about knowing the wisdom of God, then his words help you and me today to name the problems with divisive people in Christian settings so we can learn to live together in unity.

Divisive People Are . . .

First, they are "Flesh-people" (3:1, 3; *Second Testament*) because they attach themselves to *Romanitas*, the ways of life shaped for honor in the Roman city. (The NIV unfortunately translates the Greek word *sarx* as "worldly" in both 3:1 and 3:3.) Flesh for Paul is about the unredeemed person, a way of life absent of the cross and the Spirit. He wants to speak to them as "Spirit-people" (McKnight, *Second Testament*; NIV has "people who live by the Spirit" in 3:1).

Second, they are "infants in Christ." Obviously, this contrasts with the "mature" (2:6). But mature here means one who is filled with the Spirit, who walks in the way of the cross, and who lives according to the gospel. Such persons do not rip the fabric of the mission churches of Paul. Infants then points at the divisive in Corinth. To shift the expression only slightly, the problem is that they had become perpetual adolescents instead of adulting into the way of Christ.

Third, they are spirited by "zeal and strife" (McKnight, *Second Testament*), which describes their aggressive desires to acquire power and authority over the house churches in Corinth. People in churches creating zeal and strife are "Fleshies" (3:3; *Second Testament*).

Finally, they are cliquish, which reveals that, instead of deriving life from the promptings of the Spirit or having lives that conform to Christ and his cross, they are "mere human beings" (3:4). By this Paul means they are acting like unredeemed humans who are not operating in the Spirit or in God's wisdom.

Paul expects believers to grow and be transformed into mature Christians. A party spirit is no sign of maturity.

QUESTIONS FOR REFLECTION AND APPLICATION

1. How does a quest for power lead to divisiveness?

2. What is the difference between a disagreement and a division?

3. What does "flesh" mean to Paul?

4. In what ways does divisiveness reveal immaturity on the part of certain believers?

5. When have you seen a disagreement become a division in a church?

FOR FURTHER READING

Katelyn Beaty, *Celebrities for Jesus: How Personas, Platforms, and Profits Are Hurting the Church* (Grand Rapids: Brazos Press, 2022).

MINISTERS OF THE CROSS

1 Corinthians 3:5–23

⁵ *What, after all, is Apollos? And what is Paul? Only servants, through whom you came to believe—as the Lord has assigned to each his task.* ⁶ *I planted the seed, Apollos watered it, but God has been making it grow.* ⁷ *So neither the one who plants nor the one who waters is anything, but only God, who makes things grow.* ⁸ *The one who plants and the one who waters have one purpose, and they will each be rewarded according to their own labor.* ⁹ *For we are co-workers in God's service; you are God's field, God's building.*

¹⁰ *By the grace God has given me, I laid a foundation as a wise builder, and someone else is building on it. But each one should build with care.* ¹¹ *For no one can lay any foundation other than the one already laid, which is Jesus Christ.* ¹² *If anyone builds on this foundation using gold, silver, costly stones, wood, hay or straw,* ¹³ *their work will be shown for what it is, because the Day will bring it to light. It will be revealed with fire, and the fire will test the quality of each person's work.* ¹⁴ *If what has been built survives, the builder will receive a reward.* ¹⁵ *If it is burned up, the builder will suffer loss but yet will be saved—even though only as one escaping through the flames.*

¹⁶ *Don't you know that you yourselves are God's temple and that God's Spirit dwells in your midst?* ¹⁷ *If anyone destroys God's*

temple, God will destroy that person; for God's temple is sacred, and you together are that temple.

¹⁸ Do not deceive yourselves. If any of you think you are wise by the standards of this age, you should become "fools" so that you may become wise. ¹⁹ For the wisdom of this world is foolishness in God's sight. As it is written: "He catches the wise in their craftiness"; ²⁰ and again, "The Lord knows that the thoughts of the wise are futile." ²¹ So then, no more boasting about human leaders! All things are yours, ²² whether Paul or Apollos or Cephas or the world or life or death or the present or the future—all are yours, ²³ and you are of Christ, and Christ is of God.

What happens to *Romanitas*, to the ways of Rome's status-conscious life, when God's wisdom, who is Christ crucified, permeates the ones called to lead and minister in a Christian institution? This has been Paul's concern since he opened the topic at 1:18. Today's passage points out what happens and how it promotes unity and living together well. It knocks out each of the three-legged stools on which the Corinthians were sitting. People tend to exaggerate the significance of pastors, and some pastors tend to diminish the significance of the people in their church. (Notice "their" church.) Sometimes we need to flip this script because of false views of leaders and laity. Today's passage does just that. It doesn't tell us all we need to know about leaders or the people in the church. But it tells us something vital: sometimes we idolize leaders. Idolizing leaders creates toxicity. Some leaders, like Glen Campbell, want to be "where the lights are shinin' on me" ("Rhinestone Cowboy").

PERSONALITY CULTS

Today's passage begins and ends with the same concern: the names of the heads of the divisions in Corinth who claim special wisdom. Verse five mentions only Apollos and Paul, but verse twenty-two returns to the original four personalities: Paul, Apollos, Cephas. Minus one. By now it was clear that those claiming to be followers of Christ (1:12) were using him as a prop.

Charismatic preachers, leaders, teachers, and mentors tend to attract adherents. We sometimes use the term "disciples" for their followers, but we do so in a negative way. Pastors and teachers are not called to build a brand or acquire followers, nor are they to demand allegiance and loyalty. Personality cults, that is groups with leaders who create disciples of themselves, include these seven characteristics: leaders tend to be narcissists, they instill a power through a fear circle around themselves, they nurture institution creep in which the institution matters more than people, they utilize false narratives whenever an allegation arises, they demand loyalty to the leader and his inner circle, they form themselves into a celebrity culture where adoration becomes common, and instead of depicting themselves as pastors or mentors, they tend to understand themselves as leaders, entrepreneurs, and visionaries (McKnight, Barringer, *A Church Called Tov*).

That set of seven characteristics describes personality cults of all time, including the first century. More or less, that paragraph describes what was happening around Apollos and Paul, and less so probably of Cephas (Peter). If they were treating Jesus Christ in similar ways, they turned him from the Lord into a cult leader. Not impossible. Yet, we must back off thinking our passage zooms in on just leaders. Entire denominations can fit into the problem addressed in 1 Corinthians 1–3, and one could give attention to theologies (Calvinism, Wesleyanism, Stone-Campbell-ism) or movements (evangelicalism, fundamentalism).

Paul's first four chapters in this letter are designed to put leaders in their place. In so doing, he attempts to turn the lights out on the leaders and their followers. Paul moves through two phases in the heart of today's passage: he *diminishes* the significance of the leaders (3:5–15) and *elevates* the significance of the people (3:16–23). He punches *Romanitas* smack on the nose.

DIMINISHING LEADERS

Paul's question potently challenges the status quo by getting the Corinthians to ask all over again what role a leader plays in the work of God: "What [or who], after all, is Apollos? And what [or who] is Paul?" (3:5). When this letter was read aloud in the house churches, the reader paused after asking the questions and let the people in the room participate. Paul naturally answers his own questions. I want to draw your attention to three basic terms that answer these two questions of *what* is or *who* is.

First, they are *servants* in the sense that Paul and Apollos mediated the gospel to them. The Corinthians came to faith "through" them. The word behind "servants" is *diakonos*, and we get our word "deacon" from this Greek word. A servant has no authority apart from what the Lord has given to them. Paul says each servant has an assignment when he writes "as the Lord has assigned to each his task" (3:5). A servant of the Lord is called to do what the Lord has called the servant to do. The servant does not switch lanes to do the assignment of others. Youth pastors are not called to be the senior pastors, evangelism directors are not given the ministry given to the youth pastors, and professors are not assigned to the responsibilities of the provosts or presidents. Each does what the Lord calls them to do.

Second, they are *coworkers*. The emphasis from verse six through nine, though the word is not used until verse nine, is that Apollos and Paul (with Cephas) are *coworkers*. The word speaks of working alongside others. Paul describes it as one person doing one task and the other doing what comes next. A teamwork approach to discipling in the church. Paul plants a seed, and Apollos waters it. This might indicate that Paul was more the evangelist church planter, and Apollos more the church planting teacher, discipler, and mentor. But God, not Paul and not Apollos, causes the growth (3:6). Speaking of diminishing: the one planting and the one watering isn't anything—it's all about God! (3:7). As a "laborer" in God's garden, the church, each of them will be rewarded according to their assigned task (3:8). By the way, the word "labor" speaks of hard work and toil.

Third, Paul diminishes the significance of leaders when he says they are *God's grace-gifts* to the church: "By the grace God has given me" (3:10). Paul anticipates here his teaching on spiritual gifts in chapters twelve through fourteen. He doesn't name the gift *per se* and, instead, switches metaphors from gardeners to builders. Again, as coworkers, Paul lays a foundation and Apollos (presumably) built on top of it. He pauses for a pastoral reminder, looking now at anyone who plants or founds a church: the only foundation is Jesus Christ (3:11). This jabs those addicted to allegiance in one of the personality cults. Then he turns to those who build on the foundation: good resources and materials result in good buildings. Bad materials lead to a collapse on "the Day" (3:12–15). Paul, in jazz-like fashion, riffs on Jesus' parable of the wise and foolish builders (Matthew 7:24–27).

Church leaders are not celebrities, like movie and rock stars. Church leaders are like farmers and construction workers.

ELEVATING PEOPLE

In two short verses Paul informs each of us that we—together, not alone–are "God's temple" (3:16–17; "sanctuary" in *Second*

Testament). Paul concentrates special attention on God's indwelling of us as something that is plural and not singular. Of course, each of us is indwelt. However, in this passage, Paul throws all the light on the corporate indwelling of God's special presence. He wants all of us to know that we are together the dwelling place of God. God has made his home with us through the Spirit in the face of Jesus Christ. Underline how often Paul says *you* in these two verses. Each of these *you*'s is plural *you*, not singular *you*. Each is a *y'all*.

We, the temple of God, are "sacred" in our togetherness in God's presence. So sacred Paul offers the stiffest of warnings to the personality cult leaders: "If anyone destroys God's temple, God will destroy that person" (3:17). The kind of destruction such persons are doing is division, and Paul's term for destruction here can be translated as "abomination" (McKnight, *Second Testament*). The term describes corruption, degradation, corrosion, internal rot, and disruption for the sake of disruption.

Leaders are servants and coworkers assigned to tasks by God and given gifts to stay in their lane to do their task. The people are the temple of God. When persons in the institution admire and adore the leaders to the point of allegiance, God is diminished, and the glory goes to humans. Paul wants them to see that leaders are but servants doing the work of building up the church of God, not building up their brand and reputation (again, K. Beaty, *Celebrities for Jesus*).

Returning to the theme of 1:18–25 and 3:1–5, Paul finishes today's passage with summary reminders that come to their fitting finale in verse twenty-one: "So then, no more boasting about human leaders!" Actually, Paul's not so precise: "So let no one boast in humans" is all he says (McKnight, *Second Testament*). Instead of diminishing leaders, Paul diminishes *humans* because ministry is God's, not ours. Yet, we as the people of God have "all things" (3:21–22, twice).

How so? We are all "of Christ" or "Christ's" and Christ is "of God." "How freeing" (Clark-Soles, *1 Corinthians*, 15).

By God's grace.

QUESTIONS FOR REFLECTION AND APPLICATION

1. How does Paul's view of good church leaders differ from the ways many popular Christian leaders function today?

2. How might thinking of pastors as servants and coworkers instead of leaders and celebrities help build unity in the church?

3. How can elevating the significance of people in the church and diminishing the significance of leaders help disrupt divisions?

4. Of the seven characteristics of personality cult leaders, which (if any) do you notice in spiritual leaders around you?

5. Have you ever felt that a church leader looked down on you as less important? What was that experience like?

FOR FURTHER READING

Katelyn Beaty, *Celebrities for Jesus: How Personas, Platforms, and Profits Are Hurting the Church* (Grand Rapids: Brazos Press, 2022).

Scot McKnight and Laura Barringer, *A Church Called Tov* (Carol Stream: Tyndale Momentum, 2020).

"Rhinestone Cowboy." Album: *Rhinestone Cowboy.* Capitol Records, 1975. Songwriters Larry Weiss, Darren Sampson, John Matthews.

PAUL'S LEADERSHIP STYLE OF THE CROSS

1 Corinthians 4:1–21

¹ *This, then, is how you ought to regard us: as servants of Christ and as those entrusted with the mysteries God has revealed.* ² *Now it is required that those who have been given a trust must prove faithful.* ³ *I care very little if I am judged by you or by any human court; indeed, I do not even judge myself.* ⁴ *My conscience is clear, but that does not make me innocent. It is the Lord who judges me.* ⁵ *Therefore judge nothing before the appointed time; wait until the Lord comes. He will bring to light what is hidden in darkness and will expose the motives of the heart. At that time each will receive their praise from God.*

⁶ *Now, brothers and sisters, I have applied these things to myself and Apollos for your benefit, so that you may learn from us the meaning of the saying, "Do not go beyond what is written." Then you will not be puffed up in being a follower of one of us over against the other.* ⁷ *For who makes you different from anyone else? What do you have that you did not receive? And if you did receive it, why do you boast as though you did not?*

⁸ *Already you have all you want! Already you have become rich! You have begun to reign—and that without us! How I wish that you really had begun to reign so that we also might reign with*

you! ⁹ *For it seems to me that God has put us apostles on display at the end of the procession, like those condemned to die in the arena. We have been made a spectacle to the whole universe, to angels as well as to human beings.* ¹⁰ *We are fools for Christ, but you are so wise in Christ! We are weak, but you are strong! You are honored, we are dishonored!* ¹¹ *To this very hour we go hungry and thirsty, we are in rags, we are brutally treated, we are homeless.* ¹² *We work hard with our own hands. When we are cursed, we bless; when we are persecuted, we endure it;* ¹³ *when we are slandered, we answer kindly. We have become the scum of the earth, the garbage of the world—right up to this moment.*

¹⁴ *I am writing this not to shame you but to warn you as my dear children.* ¹⁵ *Even if you had ten thousand guardians in Christ, you do not have many fathers, for in Christ Jesus I became your father through the gospel.* ¹⁶ *Therefore I urge you to imitate me.* ¹⁷ *For this reason I have sent to you Timothy, my son whom I love, who is faithful in the Lord. He will remind you of my way of life in Christ Jesus, which agrees with what I teach everywhere in every church.*

¹⁸ *Some of you have become arrogant, as if I were not coming to you.* ¹⁹ *But I will come to you very soon, if the Lord is willing, and then I will find out not only how these arrogant people are talking, but what power they have.* ²⁰ *For the kingdom of God is not a matter of talk but of power.* ²¹ *What do you prefer? Shall I come to you with a rod of discipline, or shall I come in love and with a gentle spirit?*

Paul goes personal now. One could have been sitting in a house church listening to someone read this letter, and perhaps thought Paul was all done with the cliques, the cross, and ministry. Move on to something else, already! The careful listener would have realized that he was not done with that theme. Paul decides to show the Corinthians what "apostle" looks like when it has been reshaped by living a cross-shaped life. It's personal, but he's still talking about those cliques, and his aim is to form a church that lives together in unity.

To catch the pastoral heart of Paul, and not get distracted by his sarcasm, it's good to begin with the terms he uses for leaders.

LEADING AS . . .

How you see yourself, your self-image, matters. How leaders in a church or Christian institution depict and name themselves matters. The terms we use for ourselves matter—immensely. The "no one loves me because I was avoided in my family" matters just as "my coworkers and I respect one another deeply" matters.

Those with status in Corinth assigned and longed for and wore with pride labels and titles that revealed power and status. Like decurion (civic court), chief justices/magistrates, aediles and quaestors (civic manager, city treasurer), agonothete (administrator of games and festivals), and curators (of grains; Clarke, *Serve*, 41–49). Of course, most of us don't use these ancient Roman and Corinthian terms *but neither did Paul.* The only term from the political world he used was *ekklēsia*, church or assembly, which was the authoritative, political assembly of the citizens of a city. The group as a collective was given a political name, but not the persons. What is remarkable is how cross-shaped Paul's language was: he didn't choose terms of authority and power in the Roman world for leaders in the church. Voluntary associations of that world mimicked the Roman terms and did use such terms, but not the churches of Paul. They intentionally degraded their power and chose terms shaped by humility. Paul was behind it all, subverting the Corinthian claims to status title by title.

In today's passage, Paul uses three (or four) terms for himself. These terms indicate what kind of leadership Paul has in mind. The terms are "servants of Christ" (4:1), "apostles" (4:9), "fathers" (4:15), and perhaps also "guardians" (4:15). These terms describe the pastoral relation leaders have with those in their care. The first term in the NIV is "servants of Christ," but this is not the same term as the one translated "servant" in 3:5. There the term was *diakonos* but here the term is *hupēretēs*, the second term indicating a "subordinate" (*Second Testament*). That is, a lower-level responsibility in the household. Subordinate or servant has a companion in 4:1 with "those entrusted with the mysteries God has revealed" (the *oikonomos*, or "administrator"). Paul's task of going from city to city, constantly agonizing over his letters to the churches, planting a church, mentoring new elders and overseers and deacons—these tasks, and plenty more, were not exactly behind the scenes or low-level *but Paul did not want any titles of power connected to churches*. Even the term "apostle," which, for Christians today, is top of the tops, meant only a "commissioner" or one sent from some location to another with a task on behalf of someone else. His status was not "orator." In fact, "in the popular competitive sport of persuasive oratory . . . Paul was not even close to the medal stand" (Campbell, *1 Corinthians*, 73).

The third term gets emphasis: "fathers." Paul's words need to be read in full: "Even if you had ten thousand guardians in Christ, you do not have many fathers, for in Christ Jesus I became your father through the gospel. Therefore I urge you to imitate me" (4:15–16). It is noticeable that for Paul the word "father" takes precedence over "guardian" (common term for a pedagogue, mentor), and that instead of using words of instruction, he evokes the image of a son imitating, emulating, copying, mimicking his father. In chapter eleven he will say "Follow my example, as I follow the example of Christ" (11:1). He is their father, and they are his sons and daughters, and they are to observe their father and live as he lives (as he lives like Christ). Timothy was sent to them who exemplifies faithfulness. But notice this: his faithfulness exemplifies Paul's "way of life in Christ Jesus" (4:17). Since Paul is not going to be present as much as imitation required, he's sent Timothy who lives just like Paul. In the ancient world, education was about imitation and emulation more than about instruction and information. Students did not ask, "What are so-and-so's ideas?" but, "What is so-and-so's character?" The question was: Is the subordinate, the apostle, and the father worthy of emulation?

The cross of Christ transformed leadership for Paul so deeply that the terms he used needed to reflect it. He chose no terms of power and glory or celebrity. As Pheme Perkins reminds us, they are not "like the wealthy patrons who put their names on temples, amphitheaters, markets, and other public structures. Civic preferment and honor will not be theirs" (Perkins, *First Corinthians*, 83). He chose terms drawn from the registers of relationships, family, and household responsibilities. He is not done with the terms, but we need to move on before we get to his final display of what leadership meant for him.

LIVE BEFORE GOD

After informing the Corinthians that he wanted them to "regard" him as a "servant of Christ," Paul explains how servants are evaluated. They are evaluated by the household manager and owners by whether they are "faithful" to the task—whether or not they stayed in their lane to do what they were called to do (4:2). With words of evaluation flipping from one lip to another in Corinth, Paul makes it clear that he lives before God and God's evaluation, not theirs (4:3–4). He adds a commonly needed reminder: "wait until the Lord" comes for the judgment, and then we will see it is

God who judges. Not us. God's judgment is piercing and just (4:5). If you back up to the Introduction (pp. 1–16), you will see how much judging and evaluating the Corinthians were using on Paul. It takes character formed over time through some discipline and difficult days to learn to live before God and not others.

Not by Status

The problem in Corinth is found in a wonderful little word translated in the NIV as "puffed up." It is found in 4:6 but also vv. 18–19 where the NIV there translates it as "arrogant." The word means appealing to a person's "natural status" (McKnight, *Second Testament*). It evokes the claims made in Corinth by people of status, wealth, power, and property that they are to be treated specially. We will encounter this at the meals in 1 Corinthians 11 where it appears the people with some natural status ate the good food and drank the good drink and what was left over was given to the people with no status or less status. The Corinthians puffed their chests over their status and were no doubt comparing Apollos's public speaking skills with Paul's lack of such skills and background. Their claim to superiority broke faith with the reality that they were saved by grace and gifted by grace—it was all grace, it was all God, and it was not their own doing.

In spite of their puffy chests, Paul is coming, and when he comes, he will show that the "kingdom of God is not a matter of talk but of power" (4:20). Talk here is about eloquence with words and power here is about the cross in the power of God's Spirit. Their claims to status matter nothing to Paul. When he comes, they will experience him—their father, their servant, their apostle—either as a disciplinarian or as a gentle mentor who approves of their learning what it means to lead in the shadow of the cross.

REGARDLESS

Speaking of status, let's instead speak of his irritation again. Paul kind of goes off in the middle of today's passage. We should read this passage with some heat and sarcasm. The clique leaders were comparing Paul to others and Paul was losing. So, he gives them a taste of their own criticism. He uses their terms against them and does so with sharp barbs that he yanks out once he's poked them. He says they "have all" they want, and they are "rich," and they "reign," and he wished he could reign with them (sarcasm). A few lines later, Paul says they are "wise" and "strong" and "honored" while he (and others) are "fools" and "weak" and "dishonored." In fact, while he's at it he tosses some timbers on the fire. The apostles are "on display at the end of the procession . . . condemned to die in the arena" (like slaves condemned to death at the end of the parade). They are a "spectacle" for the watching crowds. He's not done: they are "hungry and thirsty, we are in rags, we are brutally treated, we are homeless. We work hard with our own hands. When we are cursed, we bless; when we are persecuted, we endure it; when we are slandered, we answer kindly." Boykin Sanders believes Paul's language here is not sarcastic but instead reveals both who the believers really are with the sad reality attached that they are not living up to who they are (supposed to be; Sanders, 1 Corinthians, 285).

Speaking of titles and labels and terms and names, he bottoms out at the end of today's passage. Remember, he has been subverting their desire for prestigious titles. Not for Paul: "We are fools for Christ." If this choice of terms is about the theatrical fool, Paul turns to the image of a buffoon for how people look at the apostle of the gospel. To the images of holy fools, like St. Francis of Assisi, or like the characters in Flannery O'Connor's short stories. And "We have become the scum of the earth, the garbage of the world." Of course, there's sarcasm and heat. Even more, there is the subversion of the clique leaders' claims to superiority and status. To make it clear, he selects terms for leaders that deny power, affirm service, and revolutionize what Christian leadership means. Charles Campbell gets it just right in writing about chapters one through four: "Paul concludes this section by subverting the status of the leaders and the assumptions of the Corinthians" (Campbell, *1 Corinthians*, 72; on holy foolishness, see 76–80).

QUESTIONS FOR REFLECTION AND APPLICATION

1. What do you see as significant in Paul's lack of using civic titles for leaders in churches?

2. How does Paul identify himself as a leader?

3. In what ways does Paul evoke familial language here for church relationships?

4. How does puffed-up pride lead to division in churches?

5. Have you ever been corrected by a church leader? Did it feel loving and transformative or shaming?

FOR FURTHER READING

Andrew Clarke, *Serve the Community of the Church: Christians as Leaders and Ministers* (Grand Rapids: Wm. B. Eerdmans, 2000).

THE ISSUES OF 1 CORINTHIANS

In reading the whole of 1 Corinthians in one sitting, one may notice the raising of a topic, its discussion and disappearance, and then another topic—rinse and repeat. Chapter five's first verse tips off the reader to know Paul is responding to a report, and it appears chapter six turns to a different topic. Chapter seven begins not by responding to a report, but to items raised in a letter. The three items found in chapters five and six could easily be attached to the eight items in chapters seven through sixteen. But it appears in one. Paul is responding to reports while in the lengthier section he has been asked about items in a letter. We have separated the two for these daily reflections, but the distinction is without much difference. One could attach the item of divisions at 1:10 and turn the whole letter into a dozen items.

Messengers from Chloe's Household

1. Division and Unity (1:10–4:21)

Reports

1. Incest (5:1–13)
2. Lawsuits (6:1–11)
3. Visiting Prostitutes (6:12–20)

Letter

1. Marriage and Status (7:1–24)
2. Virgins (7:25–40)
3. Food Sacrificed to Idols (8:1–11:1)
4. Women and Men in Worship (11:2–16)
5. The Lord's Supper (11:17–34)
6. Gifts of the Spirit (12:1–14:40)
7. Resurrection (15:1–58)
8. The Collection (16:1–11)

TOXIC BEHAVIORS IN CORINTH: (1) SEXUAL IMMORALITIES

1 Corinthians 5:1–13

[1] It is actually reported that there is sexual immorality among you, and of a kind that even pagans do not tolerate: A man is sleeping with his father's wife. [2] And you are proud! Shouldn't you rather have gone into mourning and have put out of your fellowship the man who has been doing this? [3] For my part, even though I am not physically present, I am with you in spirit. As one who is present with you in this way, I have already passed judgment in the name of our Lord Jesus on the one who has been doing this. [4] So when you are assembled and I am with you in spirit, and the power of our Lord Jesus is present, [5] hand this man over to Satan for the destruction of the flesh, so that his spirit may be saved on the day of the Lord.

[6] Your boasting is not good. Don't you know that a little yeast leavens the whole batch of dough? [7] Get rid of the old yeast, so that you may be a new unleavened batch—as you really are. For Christ, our Passover lamb, has been sacrificed. [8] Therefore let us keep the Festival, not with the old bread leavened with malice and wickedness, but with the unleavened bread of sincerity and truth.

⁹ *I wrote to you in my letter not to associate with sexually im-moral people—*¹⁰ *not at all meaning the people of this world who are immoral, or the greedy and swindlers, or idolaters. In that case you would have to leave this world.* ¹¹ *But now I am writing to you that you must not associate with anyone who claims to be a brother or sister but is sexually immoral or greedy, an idolater or slanderer, a drunkard or swindler. Do not even eat with such people.*

¹² *What business is it of mine to judge those outside the church? Are you not to judge those inside?* ¹³ *God will judge those outside. "Expel the wicked person from among you."*

Every church, eventually, will experience someone in the fellowship sinning in a way that degrades and disgraces the name of Christ. In many cases, the violations of the holiness, justice, peace, and love of the community are sexual sins. As is the case in today's passage. In the earliest churches, two types of sin expressed overt disobedience and also symbolized rejection of the ways of Christ. Those two sins were sexual sins and idolatry. No one better puts together the larger context of our passage than Jaime Clark-Soles. She observes that sexual sins are described, defined, and discussed in chapters five, six, and seven. And Paul comes at them from different angles. She paraphrases his instructions like this: "Stop having sex. Have more sex. Try not to start having sex" (Clark-Soles, *1 Corinthians*, 22). Funny, perhaps, but on-point.

What is the community to do when sexual sins are alleged? How does a church live together in unity when such sins occur? Pastoral tact requires beginning with a conversation, informing the person of what is known, learning if the report is true, concluding the report is true (or false), instructing the person in the way of Christ, pastorally caring for the person, calling the person to repent (acknowledging, confessing, turning from, setting the pattern for a righteous life), and caring for the person as he or she finds a way back to reconciliation and restoration. To be sure, each of these requires pastoral care and insight as well as patience and clarity. Public shaming of the person reveals more about those in power than about the person who has sinned, as shaming, or even the fear of shaming, in many cases will lead the person to a different church, a lawsuit, or to creating fear in the community to never tell the truth again. But sometimes, the system at work in a church or Christian institution requires public shaming for those with power to do the right thing (even if for the wrong motive and with intent of doing as little as possible).

Some persons refuse to admit the sin or to repent from the sin. In such cases, church discipline has been the church's response. Church discipline has roots in today's passage, but some of its roots have nourished puritanical toxicities, pastoral violence, abuse of authority, and defective discipleship. We must be careful to read the passage well and to practice discipline wisely. God makes us holy as a people, together and as individuals, because "Christ, our Passover lamb, has been sacrificed" (5:7). The implication is that we are to celebrate the feast of redemption with the liturgy, or daily practice, of "transparency and truth" (5:8; *Second Testament*).

THE SIN CLARIFIED

Either those from Chloe's household or Stephanas, Fortunatus, and Achaicus (16:17) informed Paul about more than those cliques. Paul opens with a very general expression to name what he has heard: sexual infidelity. If you double-click on this expression, you will be taken to the long list of sexual sins in Leviticus 18. There you will discover how ancient Israel understood sexual sin, which became the moral code for a Jewish understanding of sexual sin. But the term Paul uses is general, so he clarifies it as incest: the sexual intercourse of a man with his father's wife (probably the man's stepmother). In both Roman and Jewish law, intercourse with one's wife's mother, with one's son's wife, or one's wife's daughter or stepdaughter, or one's father's wife or one's stepmother was an outrage with stiff penalties. Incest, then, had a wide interpretation.

Elites, even if they played their hand in forming the laws and the culture, often saw themselves above and beyond the law. The wider understanding of incest was no obstacle for some. Yet, Paul appeals to the good side of the Roman laws when he writes "the kind of sexual infidelity that isn't [practiced] among the ethnic groups [gentiles]" (5:1; *Second Testament*).

THE COMMUNITY'S COMPLICITY

Not only is incest going on in the Corinthian church, but the Corinthians "are proud" (5:2). Paul's words reveal the social world of Corinth. To begin with, the word "proud" translates the Greek work *physioō*, and Paul makes it more emphatic with the perfect tense: a kind of "you have puffed yourself up." The word evokes their appealing to "natural status," that is, the incestuous couple's high social status. But the others in the assembly are doing the "boasting" (5:6). One has to ask if their pride and boasting are about, less likely, this sin in particular or, more likely, about the status of the incestuous couple. It seems reasonable, then, that the incestuous man is high status and has shacked up with a high-class woman. The incestuous couple flouted the moral standards of the gospel while at least some in the church flaunted the high-status credential of this couple. A very odd circumstance for believers in Christ.

The Corinthian workers were probably dependent on this high-class couple, and this locked them down into silence (or retaliation). What shocked Paul was their boasting about the community's and that couple's status. A sort-of *We have the biggest, best church around. Yes, our pastor's a jerk and there are rumors about his verbal abuse, power abuse, and sexual abuse. But we are still the best church around. Let's not talk about it, okay? We don't want to hurt the work of the Lord* (Clarke, *Secular and Christian,* 73–88). This is the way of Rome, that is, *Romanitas.*

Paul's words in today's reading then are aimed at the incestuous couple. He's far more concerned about how the believers are (not) responding to this explicit, public violation of Christian holiness. The whole church has become complicit, probably out of financial considerations. Their complicity expands to more sins in verse eleven where he names "greedy, an idolater or slanderer, a drunkard or swindler." The leaders in Corinth are complicit with more than incest. Whether or not the incestuous man is guilty of these sins, too, or if this list slides away from that man to others in the church, or whether he wants to make it clear that all sins corrupt the whole "batch of dough"—or all of these or some of these—his point obtains. Complicity, because of status, silence, and systemic power, needs to find the exit ramp as soon as possible.

One hears stories of leadership teams and boards ignoring, covering up, being silenced by stronger voices on the board, and spinning false narratives when allegations come forward. Paul's words are for such boards: *do the right thing. Forget reputation. Forget finances. Do the right thing. Now.*

THE ACTION NEEDED

Doing the right thing has proven to be more than difficult for those with power, for those whose reputations could be damaged, for those who could lose their job or their ministry, and for their retainers, advocates, and protectors. The Christian is called to do the right thing. What the church does makes or breaks the witness of the church.

Boykin Sanders gives the major point running through the heart of Paul's letter when he writes, "The section displays what liberation from Egypt (Roman society) means in personal and corporate terms, thus challenging the Corinthians to shake off liens against their liberation" (Sanders, *1 Corinthians*, 286). Redemption means liberation and moral transformation. What, then, was the right thing to do in Corinth? Let's assume the incestuous man knew he was wrong, and let's guess that at least one person raised an eyebrow. So, let's assume Paul didn't just jump to the end of a sound pastoral process for dealing with sin. Here are the words Paul advised: "removed from the middle of you" (5:2; *Second Testament*), "hand this man over to Satan" (5:5), "get rid of the old yeast" (5:7), and then three more: "must not associate with" and "do not even eat with" (5:11) as well as "expel" (5:13). Put together anyway you might like; the synthesis is clear: Paul wants the incestuous man removed. He does not mean believers are not to be friends with unbelievers (5:9–10).*

The key item here, however, is once again Paul is not talking to the sinful man. Paul's concern is with the church, that is, with the leadership board, and their doing the right thing. He wants them to break down their complicities, acknowledge them, and to pave a new path for the church that breaks away from letting social status, wealth, and power rule the church.

Paul's pastoral presence is promised in a most unusual way: though absent, he is present, and as Spirit-present, he has rendered a judgment on the incestuous man. When they

---

* These verses probably indicate that Paul wrote an earlier letter about dissociating from sinners and that the Corinthians misunderstood him. In the Introduction I label it "Letter A."

next gather, they are to experience Paul's presence "in spirit" but even more they are to invoke "the power of our Lord Jesus" and do the right thing (5:3–5). The right thing is not the work of human power, authority, or leadership. Church discipline that preserves the church's holiness and witness can only be done in the power of the Lord.

QUESTIONS FOR REFLECTION AND APPLICATION

1. What impact does Leviticus 18 have on the understanding of sexual sin Paul uses here?

2. How might financial dependence have impacted the Corinthian church's lack of proper response to this incestuous couple?

3. How does a whole church become complicit in one person's sin?

4. When have you seen Christian leaders or organizations look the other way in cases of egregious sin because of power or monetary considerations?

5. Are there leadership abuses in organizations you are part of that you might need to call out in light of this reading?

FOR FURTHER READING

Andrew D. Clarke, *Secular and Christian Leadership in Corinth: A Socio-Historical and Exegetical Study of 1 Corinthians 1–6* (London: Milton Keyes, 2006).

TOXIC BEHAVIORS IN CORINTH: (2) LAWSUITS AND ARBITRATION

1 Corinthians 6:1–11

¹ If any of you has a dispute with another, do you dare to take it before the ungodly for judgment instead of before the Lord's people? ² Or do you not know that the Lord's people will judge the world? And if you are to judge the world, are you not competent to judge trivial cases? ³ Do you not know that we will judge angels? How much more the things of this life! ⁴ Therefore, if you have disputes about such matters, do you ask for a ruling from those whose way of life is scorned in the church? ⁵ I say this to shame you. Is it possible that there is nobody among you wise enough to judge a dispute between believers? ⁶ But instead, one brother takes another to court—and this in front of unbelievers!

⁷ The very fact that you have lawsuits among you means you have been completely defeated already. Why not rather be wronged? Why not rather be cheated? ⁸ Instead, you yourselves cheat and do wrong, and you do this to your brothers and sisters. ⁹ Or do you not know that wrongdoers will not inherit the kingdom of God? Do not be deceived: Neither the sexually immoral nor idolaters nor adulterers nor men who have sex with men ¹⁰ nor thieves nor the greedy nor drunkards nor slanderers nor swindlers will inherit the kingdom of God. ¹¹ And that is what some of you were. But you were washed, you were sanctified, you were justified in the name of the Lord Jesus Christ and by the Spirit of our God.

For five years I, along with my wife, Kris, and daughter, Laura Barringer, have observed allegations against churches and church leaders get lodged. When allegations are made, whether going through the church processes or going public, pastors, church leaders, and boards respond with three texts. First, they appeal to Matthew 18 to contend that the alleged victim ought to go to the alleged perpetrator privately first. (No one in their right mind requires a rape or sexual assault victim to meet privately with their rapist.) Second, they appeal to 1 Timothy 5 to contend that no accusation or allegation against a pastor should be entertained unless there are, quoting the Bible's own quotation of Deuteronomy, "two or three witnesses." (Almost no sexual abuse occurs in front of witnesses.) Third, they appeal to today's text almost every time any believer chooses to go to the legal courts against a church or a pastor.

To respond to all of these at once we need to ask *Who has the advantage if a given text in Scripture is followed as the church interprets it?* Answer: the church, the pastor, the board. The appeals are rigged in favor of the church. More importantly, the use of each scripture, while it has its place, is misplaced. In some cases, I have seen colossal misuses of the Bible. In almost all cases, the intent is not to find the truth and achieve justice but to win, regardless of what happens to the one making the allegation. Usually a woman. And, finally, when scriptures like these are used, I have witnessed almost every time a significant power differential. Pastors stand for God; their victims don't. Pastors have a platform; their victims rarely do. Pastors are defended by instinct; victims are accused by instinct. The most common tactic used by pastors, boards, and churches is called DARVO: Deny (the allegation), Attack (the victim), Reverse the order of the Victim and the Offender so that the actual Victim becomes the offender, and the actual Offender makes himself (or herself) the victim.

All of this to keep us all on guard for the misuse of this text to abuse a victim who has been forced to go to court to file suit against a church she often loves more deeply than anyone in the church knows. I'm in conversation, as I write this paragraph, with two victims of pastoral abuse. Today's passage has been misused by both of those churches.

THINK ABOUT POWER AND STATUS

We will need to enter into some legal expressions in Paul's day. Since I'm not a lawyer, I'm attempting to explain the passage in a way that makes sense to me. The case of our passage occurs in a civil court, not a criminal court (6:2). Hence, the cases involved damages, fraud, contracts, or injury. Murder and physical violence are not involved. Cases in first century Corinth were ultimately determined by the political governor or by one judge. We will need to erase any idea of going before a jury of peers. The plaintiff, the one with an allegation, appeared before a magistrate who decided if there was a case, and magistrates dismissed lots of allegations. If there was a case, the magistrate brought in the defendant to hear the charges. If they stuck, the magistrate passed the case on to the judge who rendered a judgment.

Now it will take some historical thinking to train our instincts away from our modern court system. Legal privilege was systemic and based on status. That is, as one who studied the Corinthian law courts concluded, "Only those of senior status would have undertaken public litigation" (Clarke,

Secular and Christian, 62). Honor, dignity, and status mattered immensely to the magistrate and to the judge, but also to the lawyer's case. The opening case before a magistrate could lead to dismissal on the basis of status differential. The defendant's case presented before the judge was based on a defense of his client's status and reputation. All this needs to be seen so we can say going in that the "socially inferior were severely disadvantaged" and the litigant, in the case and judgment, "could greatly enhance his own reputation" (67) and damage that of the opponent. Most importantly, "these legal proceedings were being used by members of the Christian community to establish their own standing and reputation at the cost of another's" (68). Nothing is more *Romanitas*, the way of Rome, than this sense of status and privilege running the church.

So, we need to sit in this a moment. The case under review in 1 Corinthians 6 is not a trial by jury simply based on law. Instead, cases involved the status of the litigant and the defendant. Power mattered. Way too much. Today's passage is about Christian elites appearing in civil courts to defend or to establish their status. Perhaps they were suing the poor. We may proudly trumpet that our courts are more just, but we would be wise to put the trumpet down and study the statistics. Bias remains extremely influential in our courts in the USA.

SO, ARBITRATE YOUR OWN CASES

What Paul teaches here he may well have learned in the synagogue since Jewish elders often mediated disputes. Paul is not commandeering *criminal* law from the public sector to the church. In our passage, Paul calls the issues in dispute "trivial cases" and "the things of this life" (6:2, 3). He diminishes the significance of what is in dispute. The case at hand was a civil case, and Paul knew enough about how the system worked to warn believers about complicity in corruptions. Most importantly, Paul pushes against the bias toward status and power as he urges for a more church-based egalitarian, even democratic, approach to resolving disputes. His radical edge shows up in diminishing the power of the powerful and turning cases over to the ordinaries of a church. In which case, status collapses and the poor are raised to the same level as those with status. Siblings can judge siblings, regardless of their status. It would be foolish to think Paul was legislating the formation of case law within a church. He had an angle on disputes between siblings that he believed could achieve greater justice. As Charles Campbell phrases it, "The hierarchical arrangements of Corinthian society . . . are overturned in the Christian community" (Campbell, *1 Corinthians*, 104).

Mark each question in today's reading. Then read it aloud with a long pause at the end of each question. In the pause, imagine the audience of this letter listening and responding to each question.

First, he contends that unbelievers will be biased against the believers. He calls those in the court system "wrongdoers" (6:1, 9; *Second Testament*; NIV has "ungodly"*), the "world" (6:2), and "unbelievers" (6:6). With "the devalued in the assembly" (6:4; *Second Testament*; NIV has "those whose way of life is scorned in the church") Paul makes it clear that those sitting in judgment have no respect with believers. One has to think the unbelievers' worldviews and moral instincts are out of line with the worldview and moral instincts of believers. How many times have we watched a case and muttered to ourselves or to others that *the court decision may well have been according to law, but it was not morally right.*

---

* The Greek word belongs to the court: *adikos* means "unjust" or "one who does what is wrong."

Campbell again: "The Body of Christ operates differently from the body politic" (Campbell, *1 Corinthians*, 105).

Second, for each of these labels for unbelievers Paul uses a contrasting idea or term for believers because he believes they are different. So, he calls those in the church "the devoted ones" (6:1; *Second Testament*; NIV has "the Lord's people" for the simple word "holy ones" or "saints" or "devoted ones"), "brothers" (6:6) but most especially he uses "you" and "we" for those in the faith. He contends believers, lit up as they can be in the Spirit, have a higher competence: they will render judgment on the world and angels (6:2, 3; cf. Daniel 7:22; 2 Peter 2:4), and there are those in their midst who are "wise" (6:5).

Third, Paul cuts through the entire city of Corinth by declaring who is "in" the kingdom and who is "out." He points to those regenerated by the Spirit into the way of Christ: those who are "washed" and "sanctified" and "justified" (6:11). Those who will not enter the kingdom enact the notorious sins of gentile sinners, that is, those sinners Paul has observed on the streets of Corinth (and probably Ephesus as well): "Neither the sexually immoral nor idolaters nor adulterers nor men who have sex with men* nor thieves nor the greedy nor drunkards nor slanderers nor swindlers will inherit the kingdom of God" (6:9–10). The church of Corinth was small; the Christian movement was one generation old; the moral problems challenging; and the

---

* Translating any term connected with male-male relations requires sensitivity. The language Paul uses is graphic: "males being penetrated [by males] nor [males] penetrating males" (*Second Testament*). More literally, the first term (*malakos*) refers to the male who receives from another male, while the second term (*arsenokoitēs*) refers to a male going to bed with another male. Paul knows the same-sex realities of the Roman world, which encompassed pederasty and gross sexual indulgences. It is unlikely Paul speaks here of monogamous, consensual relations. His language is stereotypical for the notorious sins of notorious sinners drawn from the Jewish moral codes.

solutions were experimental as the church grew into its own traditions. Many denominations today have their own "ecclesiastical" courts, which are modeled on public court systems but adapted to moral and church disputes. What Paul knew was that the law courts were status-based, that high-status believers would be asserting status in the courts more than pursuing justice (the point of 6:7–8), and that believers ought to be able to arbitrate their own disputes.

There is a time for believers to meet with one another to settle disputes; there is a time for them to be guided by a mediator; and, at times, there will be times to go to court. The smaller the case, the more it should be handled outside the courts. The more legally challenging the case, the more the need for going to court becomes necessary. In all cases, believers ought not to be flaunting their status and wealth and power or flouting the laws of the land. The sad history of churches proves flouting law has come home to roost.

QUESTIONS FOR REFLECTION AND APPLICATION

1. How can and has today's passage been used against victims of abuse?

2. What light does this study of Corinthian courts shed on interpreting this passage?

3. How do the differences in values and culture between church people and secular people play into Paul's advice here?

4. How might status have impeded justice in the civil courts of Paul's day?

5. When are there times today that Christians going to court might be a better option than trying to settle things internally in the church?

FOR FURTHER READING

Andrew D. Clarke, *Secular and Christian Leadership in Corinth: A Socio-Historical and Exegetical Study of 1 Corinthians 1–6* (London: Milton Keyes, 2006).

TOXIC BEHAVIORS IN CORINTH: (3) VISITING PROSTITUTES

1 Corinthians 6:12–20

[12] "I have the right to do anything," you say—but not everything is beneficial. "I have the right to do anything"—but I will not be mastered by anything. [13] You say, "Food for the stomach and the stomach for food, and God will destroy them both." The body, however, is not meant for sexual immorality but for the Lord, and the Lord for the body. [14] By his power God raised the Lord from the dead, and he will raise us also. [15] Do you not know that your bodies are members of Christ himself? Shall I then take the members of Christ and unite them with a prostitute? Never! [16] Do you not know that he who unites himself with a prostitute is one with her in body? For it is said, "The two will become one flesh." [17] But whoever is united with the Lord is one with him in spirit.

[18] Flee from sexual immorality. All other sins a person commits are outside the body, but whoever sins sexually, sins against their own body. [19] Do you not know that your bodies are temples of the Holy Spirit, who is in you, whom you have received from God? You are not your own; [20] you were bought at a price. Therefore honor God with your bodies.

"I grew up," a woman in our church said to me one day in the sanctuary, "being told my body does not matter. It's nothing but flesh. What matters is my spirit." She asked, "Is that what Paul means by 'flesh'—the body as body, the body as bad?" No, that idea is not Paul's. For Jews, the body, the spirit, and the soul are one—but not for Greeks floating along the current shaped by Plato, and not for those in the Roman world who had been influenced by Plato and his successors. In fact, many would say Jews mostly did not accept dualism: we are embodied souls or soul-ish bodies. Not body *and* soul. Not two, but one. For some in Corinth, bodies ranked below the spirit and the soul, and what mattered most was the soul. What one did with one's body did not matter.

BODIES MATTER

I want to begin where Paul's thoughts actually begin, with the body that matters. Notice this statement: "The body" is meant "for the Lord, and the Lord for the body" (6:13). I cannot come close to stating how utterly nonsensical that would have been for some Corinthians. Paul's not done, for he writes, "your bodies are members of Christ himself" (6:15). As bodies unite in sexual union, so the believer's body "is united with the Lord" and is thus "one with him in spirit" (6:17). A few more now: "your bodies are temples of the Holy Spirit" and the Holy Spirit is "in" your body and your body "is not your own" but your body was "bought at a price" and you are to "honor God with your bodies" (6:18–20). Yes, I have touched up Paul's words by adding body here and there but only because the word is assumed.

Your body. Every pound you weigh. Every hair on your body. Every inch of skin and nails and your teeth, and eyes and ears and nose, and lips and knees and toes. Your body matters because your body is you, and you are your body. It is imperfect, and someday will be perfected, which is what Paul says in 1 Corinthians 15. But you are not without your body. You may not take care of it as you ought, and you may obsess over it more than you ought, and you may be depressed about its aging—but it is you. It is not something you possess but something you are.

Bodies matter so much Paul says union with a prostitute is a sacred embodied action that forms a union with that person. In the Corinthian world, males especially were known for procreational sex at home with one's wife and recreational sex with one's enslaved woman, with prostitutes who were everywhere available and not looked down upon, and for some with boys or other men. Surely, one of the most radical dimensions of earliest believers' way of life, which was carried with them from the law of Moses, was sexual faithfulness to one's wife (or husband). Sex was a one-man and one-woman consensual act, and it lasted as long as one's marriage lasted. (The next chapter enters into this topic.) Bodies matter. Sex with another person is an embodied sacred act of union. To enter into that union implied and required rights and duties with and to one another.

RATIONALIZATIONS ARE RATIONALIZATIONS

Why people choose to do what they do remains below the surface. Even unconscious to the person. But what erupts from the surface reveals the inner world. If not the inner world, at least a rationalization. Today's passage opens with rationalization of a person's desire, and by "desire" I mean sexual pleasures and their lusty urges. Some in Corinth— and the italics in the NIV tip off that the translators think Paul is quoting someone else's words—claimed their "rights" or permissibilities to do "all things" with their bodies. Such persons must think their bodies don't matter. (Paul counters that not everything is "beneficial" and that we should not be "mastered by anything"; 6:12). And food and the stomach matter not a bit because God's gonna destroy them someday.

The inference such a person draws is that they can do whatever they want with the body—prostitution and gluttony mean nothing. Paul recognizes the logic for what it is: rationalization of the lusty desires of indulgence. Plus, really bad theology. Plato and Moses, with the prophets and Jesus and Paul, do not get along well when it comes to bodies. People want to do what they want to do, and they are skilled at finding reasons for what they want. Rationalizations remain rationalizations.

SEXUAL PARTNERS MATTER TO GOD

To live together well as believers in Jesus at times requires clarifying Christian sexual ethics. Chapters five through seven have lots of sexual ethics in them. Today's passage is for many of us the low point because of what it reveals about the men of Corinth who claim to be followers of Jesus. They not only degrade their bodies, but also, they participate in the commercialization of a woman's body. Women then and today are sometimes driven to prostitution in their desperation. As Jaime Clark-Soles says it so well, "Using the bodies of others, and especially those who have no choice, is incommensurate with the Logic of Love" (Clark-Soles, *1 Corinthians*, 26).

Paul's move then from the voluntary incest of chapter five to the prostitutes of chapter six is a shift to one of the sordid realities of Corinth. As Pheme Perkins graphically depicts the chapter shift and ridicules the beastly behaviors of the men, when Paul "shifts to brothels, *porneia* [sexual infidelity] is no longer high-profile incest but the hoglike snorting and grunting coming from rooms around the local baths" (Perkins, *1 Corinthians*, 86). The bath houses of Corinth and Pompeii and Rome and Ephesus alike degraded the women and unmasked the character of the men engaged with the women.

The body matters, it is designed for the Lord, and in the body the Spirit dwells, as Paul has already said. Those are his flashpoints. So, Paul orders the Corinthians to "flee from sexual immorality" because it's a sin of the body and against the body (6:18). As Gordon Fee puts it, that body may be "his own but not his own"! (Fee, *First Corinthians*, 288). His explanation may surprise because he makes sexual sin a singular sin: "All other sins a person commits are outside the body, but whoever sins sexually, sins against their own body" (6:18). I'm wondering, and perhaps you are too, what Paul means. Is not gluttony an embodied sin, too? Is he thinking of Genesis 2 where woman comes from man and that a man's sin with a prostitute violates his Adamic origins? Or perhaps "every sin (NIV has "all other sins" but that's not accurate; it says all sins) a person commits is outside the body" is quoting the person who also said "I have the right to do anything" I want in verse twelve. Paul then in the second clause counters that false idea with "but whoever sins sexually, sins against their own body" (6:18). I'm inclined to think this is the best explanation, but we can't be sure.

We can be sure that for Paul the body matters because it is the habitation of God's Spirit and that we are responsible to worship God with our bodies. Bodies matter. Therefore, sexual unions matter.

QUESTIONS FOR REFLECTION
AND APPLICATION

1. How much do you think your body matters?

2. How does a lack of valuing the body lead to prostitution in Corinth?

3. In what ways does Paul conceptually relate worship and sexual sin?

4. Have we in the Western world flipped the first century script to where bodies matter but the soul/spirit no longer matters?

5. Do you notice any body/soul dualism in your thinking?

LETTER ITEM #1: MARRIAGE

1 Corinthians 7:1–40

[1] Now for the matters you wrote about: "It is good for a man not to have sexual relations with a woman." [2] But since sexual immorality is occurring, each man should have sexual relations with his own wife, and each woman with her own husband. [3] The husband should fulfill his marital duty to his wife, and likewise the wife to her husband. [4] The wife does not have authority over her own body but yields it to her husband. In the same way, the husband does not have authority over his own body but yields it to his wife. [5] Do not deprive each other except perhaps by mutual consent and for a time, so that you may devote yourselves to prayer. Then come together again so that Satan will not tempt you because of your lack of self-control. [6] I say this as a concession, not as a command. [7] I wish that all of you were as I am. But each of you has your own gift from God; one has this gift, another has that.

[8] Now to the unmarried and the widows I say: It is good for them to stay unmarried, as I do. [9] But if they cannot control themselves, they should marry, for it is better to marry than to burn with passion.

[10] To the married I give this command (not I, but the Lord): A wife must not separate from her husband. [11] But if she does, she

must remain unmarried or else be reconciled to her husband. And a husband must not divorce his wife.

¹² To the rest I say this (I, not the Lord): If any brother has a wife who is not a believer and she is willing to live with him, he must not divorce her. ¹³ And if a woman has a husband who is not a believer and he is willing to live with her, she must not divorce him. ¹⁴ For the unbelieving husband has been sanctified through his wife, and the unbelieving wife has been sanctified through her believing husband. Otherwise your children would be unclean, but as it is, they are holy.

¹⁵ But if the unbeliever leaves, let it be so. The brother or the sister is not bound in such circumstances; God has called us to live in peace. ¹⁶ How do you know, wife, whether you will save your husband? Or, how do you know, husband, whether you will save your wife?

¹⁷ Nevertheless, each person should live as a believer in whatever situation the Lord has assigned to them, just as God has called them. This is the rule I lay down in all the churches. ¹⁸ Was a man already circumcised when he was called? He should not become uncircumcised. Was a man uncircumcised when he was called? He should not be circumcised. ¹⁹ Circumcision is nothing and uncircumcision is nothing. Keeping God's commands is what counts. ²⁰ Each person should remain in the situation they were in when God called them.

²¹ Were you a slave when you were called? Don't let it trouble you—although if you can gain your freedom, do so. ²² For the one who was a slave when called to faith in the Lord is the Lord's freed person; similarly, the one who was free when called is Christ's slave. ²³ You were bought at a price; do not become slaves of human beings. ²⁴ Brothers and sisters, each person, as responsible to God, should remain in the situation they were in when God called them.

²⁵ Now about virgins: I have no command from the Lord, but I give a judgment as one who by the Lord's mercy is trustworthy. ²⁶ Because of the present crisis, I think that it is good for a man to

remain as he is. *27 Are you pledged to a woman? Do not seek to be released. Are you free from such a commitment? Do not look for a wife. 28 But if you do marry, you have not sinned; and if a virgin marries, she has not sinned. But those who marry will face many troubles in this life, and I want to spare you this.*

29 What I mean, brothers and sisters, is that the time is short. From now on those who have wives should live as if they do not; 30 those who mourn, as if they did not; those who are happy, as if they were not; those who buy something, as if it were not theirs to keep; 31 those who use the things of the world, as if not engrossed in them. For this world in its present form is passing away.

32 I would like you to be free from concern. An unmarried man is concerned about the Lord's affairs—how he can please the Lord. 33 But a married man is concerned about the affairs of this world— how he can please his wife—34 and his interests are divided. An unmarried woman or virgin is concerned about the Lord's affairs: Her aim is to be devoted to the Lord in both body and spirit. But a married woman is concerned about the affairs of this world—how she can please her husband. 35 I am saying this for your own good, not to restrict you, but that you may live in a right way in undivided devotion to the Lord.

36 If anyone is worried that he might not be acting honorably toward the virgin he is engaged to, and if his passions are too strong and he feels he ought to marry, he should do as he wants. He is not sinning. They should get married. 37 But the man who has settled the matter in his own mind, who is under no compulsion but has control over his own will, and who has made up his mind not to marry the virgin—this man also does the right thing. 38 So then, he who marries the virgin does right, but he who does not marry her does better.

39 A woman is bound to her husband as long as he lives. But if her husband dies, she is free to marry anyone she wishes, but he must belong to the Lord. 40 In my judgment, she is happier if she stays as she is—and I think that I too have the Spirit of God.

A t times in the history of the church, some enthusiastic believers have decided the situation calls for celibacy. Like those in monasteries, like priests in the Catholic and Orthodox tradition (if they were unmarried when they were ordained), or like the Shakers. The situations for these were not identical. For some, the situation was devotion to the Lord, the church, and ministry. For others, the situation was conviction, so far always mistaken, that the return of Christ was imminent and called for drastic measures. Evidently, in Corinth some believers came to believe they were called to celibacy and were pressuring others to enter into a life of celibacy. What a strange church, you may be muttering, some incest, some visiting of brothels, and some celibates. Sex—good. No sex—superior. Sex—inferior. Let's have sex, let's not have sex.

This long chapter addresses marriage for believers who believe the time is short and who want to be fully devoted to the Lord before his imminent return. We can look at the entire chapter through ten principles. Today's passage does not offer much wisdom about Christian marriage *per se*. Instead, the passage opens for us a window on an enthusiastic moment in the Corinthian church where some were deciding if marriage was compatible with total devotion to the Lord. The unusualness of the situation ought to guide us to cautious uses of this chapter, but the situation did provoke Paul to think carefully about marriage and the Christian life.

PAUL ON HIS OWN

Four times in today's passage Paul distinguishes himself from the Lord, his teachings from the Lord's words. At times, he repeats what Jesus taught; at other times he adds to what Jesus taught; at other times he's on his own. In no case does he disagree with what Jesus taught. In our first example, in 7:8, Paul only says "I say" but once we read 7:10, 12, and 25, we realize his "I say" is also a "not the Lord." Paul knows the teachings of Jesus, which has been preserved in part for us in Matthew 5:31–32 and 19:1–12. Jesus taught the permanence of the marriage covenant; the permissibility of divorce in the case of sexual immorality by one partner; and the possibility of celibacy ("eunuchs for the sake of the kingdom").

Not only does he distinguish Jesus' words from his own, but Paul divulges that (at least) some of what he offers in this chapter is his opinion. Notice "I *order* thus in all the assemblies" (7:17; *Second Testament*; NIV uses the word "rule"),* and since he can't appeal to an "order" from the Lord he offers to them his considered "conclusion" (7:25, 40; *Second Testament*; NIV: "judgment"). Does it not appear to you that Paul is presenting his "best, practical attempt to answer the Corinthians' conundrums"? (Campbell, *1 Corinthians*, 119). Boykin Sanders labels these bits of advice from Paul "concessionary considerations" (Sanders, *1 Corinthians*, 289).

Paul encounters in his mission new situations in the churches. Along with marriage and celibacy, he discovers that some want to divorce unbelievers because they are unbelievers; that some want to change their status, that is from married to unmarried; that some think celibacy is for all and that others wonder if it's okay to marry. When Jesus had spoken, Paul sided with Jesus. When Jesus had not spoken, Paul discerned in the Spirit what was best. As he puts it, "I think that I too have the Spirit of God" (7:40).

What is clear is that this is not about communal discernment; what we read here is Paul's discernment. Many who use this passage for communal discernment end up doing

---

* What Paul means by "order" is that he offers to them an organizing principle that provides structure for the churches.

exactly what Paul did not do: lay down the law. Some in communal discernment form what they would say is a "consensus," which usually means the more authoritative voices have "won," and then expect all to go along with the consensus. What happens in 1 Corinthians 7 (take a good hard look at 11:16) is not expecting everyone to go along with Paul but to hear him out. He thinks he's right. He doesn't tell them what to do so much as give his advice (Fee, *First Corinthians*). Many would say he gives them the agency to decide in light of his conclusions.

At times, Paul was on his own, and at times, we are too. Paul obviously did not think Jesus, or the Bible, had covered every topic with clarity. What he teaches when he goes on his own has not been, for instance, the teaching of the vast majority of Protestants. In the history of the church, what Paul seems to be offering in chapter seven is called *adiaphora*, matters of discussion and discernment but which do not rise to the level of essential teachings. At the end of that most-debated section in 1 Corinthians 11, Paul closes down the discussion with a humble word for all of us: "If anyone wants to be contentious about this [what he wrote in vv. 2–15]," and I translate "we don't have any such custom [about this]" (11:16; NIV with *Second Testament*).

Paul clearly knows when his opinions need to be distinguished from rock-solid gospel truths. What Jesus says is one thing; what Paul says is another.

LIVING IN THE "AS IF"

The first generation of believers, among whom was Paul, had moments when it not only wondered and hoped for but believed the return of Christ was right around the corner. Paul refers to this situation when he calls it "the present crisis" (7:26), but in 7:29–31 he develops this. Not only with "the time is short" or tightened, compressed, but also with "this world in its present form is passing away" (7:31). An "as if" ethic can be understood (and is by some) as an "other-worldly stance" (Sanders, *1 Corinthians*, 290).

In the conviction that Christ's return is imminent, Paul calls for an "as if" way of life. Again, his concern is celibacy, here expressed as "Now about virgins" (7:25).* They become for Paul a model of the "as if" life. That is, the married are to live "as if" they are not, the mourners "as if" they are not, the happy "as if" they are not, and those who buy something "as if it were not theirs to keep." Paul clearly affirms the "better" status of a celibate life, and in this "as if" section the celibate life influences the married, the happy, and the possessions life.

How this looked in a home is not clear but the angle on life is redemptive: *living in light of the soon return of Christ can deepen our commitment to the Lord.* As long as we don't get nutso and start predicting the times and dates. As long as we don't neglect the constant realities of life. Even this principle has an angle for Paul, which leads to our next one.

Groups Addressed in 1 Corinthians 7

1. Married (vv. 1–7)
2. Unmarried (celibates) and widows (vv. 8–9)
3. Married (10–11)
4. Those with unbelieving partners (12–16)
5. Virgins (celibates, not yet married) (25–38)
6. Married women and widows (39–40)

---

* In the letter sent to Paul (7:1), it is likely someone asked if, in the present crisis and the imminent coming of the Lord, singles should get married, which led to the section from 7:25–40.

CELIBACY IS "BETTER" THAN MARRIAGE

Whether we like it or not, Paul makes his angle clear: "So then, he who marries the virgin does right, but he who does not marry her does better" (7:38). His belief in the superior life of the celibate, again in that situation, shapes the entire passage.

Some in Corinth took Paul's ideas about celibacy to an extreme and were acclaiming that it was superior for a man "not to touch a woman" (7:1), with the "touch" a metaphor for sexual intercourse. In the next verse, Paul counters that sexual intercourse is perfectly fine for a married couple. Jaime Clark-Soles states Paul's view perfectly: "ditch the contrived restraint and enjoy God's good creation" (Clark-Soles, *1 Corinthians*, 27). In fact, each is instructed to focus on the pleasure of the other, and he informs the married men in Corinth to consider first the pleasure of their wives. So much so that he flips the entire social script when he writes that "the husband does not have authority over his own body but yields it to his wife" (7:4). One has to think Paul is affirming here the fundamental importance of consent and mutuality in all sexual connections. He also affirms agency on the part of women.

But he believes sexual relations in a marriage are a "concession" and not a "command" (7:6). He quickly adds that he wishes everyone was "as I am," that is, celibate (7:7 and 7:8). He encourages widows to remain unmarried, that is, celibate (7:40). The apostle was a celibate who thought the celibate life was the better way to live as a Christian. He didn't demand it, but he advised it while giving each person freedom to decide.

The passage that opens today's reading has been abused, mostly by married men who demand sexual relations with their wife because Paul teaches they are not to deprive one another. But he also believes in "mutual consent" celibacy "for a time," in spiritual practices taking precedence, and in the need for sexual relations in order to avoid temptation (7:5–6). Sex-to-avoid-temptation probably reflects the opinion of a celibate, and there would have been some to say this theory is incomplete. Again, all of this can be easily abused when one partner demands sex. When demanding is at work, a problem is revealed that ought to lead straight to the therapist's office.

Even with this wisdom we need to remind ourselves that in that crisis situation with some thinking, including Paul, Christ was about to return, Paul thought celibacy was a superior life. The church has respected this point of view but has also concentrated its teachings on the permissibility of marriage and what a Christian marriage best looks like.

Paul's words form in the register of sex and celibacy along with marriage. In one column next to that register we find singleness, which is both devalued in much of the evangelical and Protestant world and in need of fresh revival for those so called by the Lord (cf. 7:7). In a recent Substack by the writer Katelyn Beaty about her single, and flourishing, life, she offers words that may well speak deep truths to many:

I thought that if I didn't have the thing, then I wouldn't be happy.

Here's the thing: If you can't be happy without the thing—the job, the house, the wardrobe, the vacation, the baby, the sex life, the friendship, the social media following, the 401k, the dynamic church—then you won't be happy even if you get it.

If you can't see your life for the blessing that it is—in its actual, on-the-ground, moment-to-moment unfolding, with all its unmet longings and griefs and discomfort and boredom—then you won't see the blessing even when your longing is met or your grief subsides or perhaps you find incredible joy with another person in this life. (Beaty, "I had to leave . . .")

Much needs to be said, taught, and written about singleness, including the sometimes idolization of marriage, the struggle others have with singleness, and the struggle singles have with marrieds and churches out of sync with singles.

Author and researcher Sheila Wray Gregoire does important work helping Christian couples realize that obligation sex is not God's plan for marriage. If someone feels forced to have sex they don't want in their marriage, they should seriously consider whether they are being sexually abused. In a blog post about 1 Corinthians 7, she writes:

Any claim that he has over her body is matched by the claim that she has over his, which means that neither of us can use our bodies in ways that the other doesn't want.

The point of this passage is not to say that the husband can use his wife's body, and she has no rights to it. The point of this passage is not about one person being able to overpower the other.

The point of this passage is that sex should always and only ever be mutual.

The idea of a wife having authority over her husband's body was the revolutionary part.

We focus so much in the church in telling women that they don't have authority over their own bodies, but instead they give that authority to their husbands.

Do you realize that in doing so, we're doing the exact OPPOSITE of what Paul was trying to do in this passage?

In the context that Paul was writing, husbands already had authority over their wives' bodies. In fact, it went further than that. They owned their wife's body, to the extent that they could kill them and not face punishment.

When Paul wrote, "The wife does not have authority over her own body but yields it to her husband," everybody would have said, "Well, D'UH!" Of course that's true!

But then we get to those four revolutionary words: In the same way . . . (in Greek it's not four words, but you know what I mean!).

That would have shocked his readers. Wives didn't have any authority over their husbands at all, and yet here Paul is saying, *whatever authority husbands have over their wives' bodies is matched by the authority that God gives wives over their husbands' bodies.*

Paul is saying that men no longer have the upper hand. Men can't just use their wives. No, instead Paul is equalizing things and insisting that mutuality rather than obligation and force be the principle in sexual relations. If she has claims to his body in the same way that he has claims to hers, then he can't use her. He can't do anything she doesn't want. Paul is equalizing things!

And yet, instead of understanding Paul's intention here, *we have used 1 Corinthians 7:3–5 to put women in the exact same position that Paul was fighting against.* We have completely ignored the context and the principle behind what he was saying, and focused merely on one phrase. And it has done tremendous damage.

https://baremarriage.com/2022/11/1-corinthians-7
-sexual-autonomy/
See *The Great Sex Rescue* by Sheila Wray Gregoire,
Rebecca Gregoire Lindenbach, and Joanna
Sawatsky for more.

FREE FOR DEVOTION, FREE FROM DISTRACTION

A life of celibacy made possible a life of devotion to the Lord
and a life freer from the distractions of life. The married, Paul
claims, "will face many troubles in this life" (7:28). The NIV's
translation shapes it one way but a more literal reading is "Such
persons will have trouble in the flesh" (McKnight, *Second
Testament*). Paul is giving advice here (Fee, *First Corinthians*,
368). He's not laying down the law. Flesh troubles could be dif-
ficulties with one's passions, but marriage seems to take care
of that for Paul (7:9). We do know the troubles are connected
to the present crisis (7:26). The next passage, so I believe,
clarifies what the flesh-trouble is. The most radically celibate
idea Paul presents is his "as if" lines in 7:29–31. He seems to
think married couples can live together, sleep together, and
love one another, but do life "as if" they are not married. His
teaching is aimed at the men, but the women experience the
same convoluted set of ideas. The way to maintain devotion
to the Lord and freedom from distraction is to live together as
celibates. Oy. Only a successfully celibate man can think such
thoughts. And good for such celibates. Most couples who try
this don't last. And most couples who are celibate, well, are
probably not doing as well as they ought to be.

The celibate man, and Paul is one, "is concerned about
the Lord's affairs" but the married man, and Paul is not

one, is "concerned about the affairs of this world," by which he means pleasing his wife (7:32–33). This passage stings because too many men are so dedicated to their profession, they neglect their wives. There is nothing wrong with pleasing one's wife, and Paul knows this because he knows marriage is good. Yet, he thinks celibacy is better and that is why he writes what he does in these verses. He knows that at least some celibates can live in those pressing times "in undivided devotion to the Lord" (7:35). Some women in the early church took Paul's word for it and went for it: they became gospelers and teachers and missionaries and church planters. Names like Thecla and Felicitas. (Google them.)

MARRIAGE IS RESPECTABLE

I waited for this principle so we moderns who believe in marriage—along with most in the church—will experience the celibacy ideas of Paul at work in today's passage. It is honorable and respectable for a woman and a man to be married and to enjoy the embodied pleasures of life together (7:36–38). Paul has already conceded this (7:1–7, esp. 7:6) and he develops this concession in vv. 36–38. Passions are to be respected, that is, the passions leading to marriage. But again, marriage is respected even if it remains a concession for Paul, the celibate. Celibacy is "better" (7:38).

MARRIAGE IS PERMANENT

Once you get married, it's permanent. Paul knows Jesus' teachings, but he expands or extends his teachings here. That's suggested by "not I, but the Lord" (7:10). In the context of Corinth some women seem to have wanted to divorce their husbands, perhaps in order to devote themselves more fully to the Lord. Paul prohibits, like Jesus, such a divorce.

(This would not prohibit divorces in cases of abuse, abandonment, or sexual immorality.) And if she does divorce, she must either become a celibate or reunite with her former husband (7:11). The man, too, must not divorce his wife—again repeating Jesus' teachings. When her partner dies, she is "free to marry anyone she wishes" as long as the man is a believer (7:39). Paul the celibate's "judgment" is that she would be "blessed" (McKnight, *Second Testament*; NIV has "happier") if she remains a celibate (7:40).

REMAINING IN ONE'S SITUATION

Paul spends some energy in our passage on instructing believers to "remain in the situation they were in when God called them" to himself in Christ (7:20, 24). The circumcised are not to go through the procedure, called *epispasm*, of reversing their condition; the uncircumcised don't need to be circumcised. Neither of those conditions matters (7:17–20). He extends his teaching to enslaved persons. "Don't let it be a concern to you" (7:21; *Second Testament*). With a possibly profound concession that, if the opportunity arises to be emancipated, they are to "do so" (7:21). He flips the script of slavery: one enslaved to a human is actually in Christ now "the Lord's freed person," and the formerly freed person is now a "slave" to Christ (7:22). With the script flipped he orders all of them never to become "slaves of human beings" (7:23). Having said that, it is a fact that the Bible never overtly condemns, denounces, or even disapproves of slavery as an institution. We must be willing to consider that the cultural blinders of the age blinded the apostle Paul, and others, from the immorality of slavery. It would take centuries even for the church to come to a more Christian understanding of slavery.

The shift from marriage, sex, and celibacy to circumcision, uncircumcision, and enslavement requires us to ponder these as illustrations of his teachings about marriage and celibacy. If they are married, remain married; if they are celibate, remain celibate. The time is short, and they can last as they serve the Lord with holy ardor.

Two principles are advised briefly for the impact of a believer on a non-believer in a mixed marriage.

BELIEVER SANCTIFIES PARTNER

Paul knows his next teaching is a "not the Lord" teaching. He discerns that a believer, who is sanctified in Christ through the Spirit (6:11), (1) ought not to divorce the unbeliever because (2) the unbelieving partner is "sanctified," which here means brought closer to the Lord or devoted to the Lord by the believing partner (7:13–14). And, (3) otherwise "the children would be unclean," and that's not possible for the apostle Paul. Paul affirms here the covenant relationship of God with God's people, and consequently for the children of God's people. In today's churches, children are either baptized into the covenanted community or dedicated. Either way, parents express their faith on behalf of their children and their children's future spiritual development. We are left wondering what it looks like to sanctify a partner or a child. Perhaps wondering is all we can do as we ponder what it would look like in our families and in mixed marriages.

BELIEVER SAVES PARTNER

It's not Paul's strategy but it has been for many women and men in the history of the church. That is, a woman marries a man in the hope and prayers that he will turn his life over to the Lord Jesus. Salvation happens. Sometimes. But not always. Paul urges believers not to divorce unbelieving partners because the opportunity to "save" the person will be forfeited by divorce (7:15–16). Again, watch out for this one. Some unbelieving spouses are abusive (and so are some spouses professing belief), and this passage does not address abusive spouses. Nor would Paul teach remaining with them in an abusive situation. If the unbeliever wants to leave, "let it be so" (7:15). But divorce is not recommended. Would Paul permit remarriage? Yes, but don't be surprised if you then think *but he'd prefer celibacy.*

TWO MORE PRINCIPLES

Already at work in most of the principles above, are that *sexual relations*, no matter how good and vital to a couple's relationship, *are subordinate to celibacy* (7:1–7, 8, 38, 40) and *the decision to marry and to enjoy marital relations are subordinate to losing control* (7:9).

From the top of this passage to the bottom, Paul's assumes and builds upon his practice and belief in celibacy as the "better" way of life during the "present crisis" as this world is "passing away." If one does not affirm his view of celibacy, and Paul clearly knows in this passage and others in 1 Corinthians that his view is his view and not always held by the Lord or by all, some of what he says will need to be shifted. Celibacy, I believe, needs to be understood as Jesus understood it, which Paul echoes when he writes that "each of you has your own gift from God; one has this gift, another has that" (7:7).

QUESTIONS FOR REFLECTION AND APPLICATION

1. How does Paul distinguish his own words and advice from those of the Lord?

2. What example does Paul set here of discernment for cultural situations extrapolated from the words of Jesus?

3. How normative do you think Paul intends his teachings in this passage to be?

4. How does Paul emphasize consent and mutuality in married sex?

5. What could the church do today to better support single Christians and those committed to celibacy?

FOR FURTHER READING

Katelyn Beaty, "I had to leave the Christian suburbs to thrive as a single woman," at: https://katelynbeaty.substack.com/p/christian-suburbs-wheaton-marriage-single-woman

LETTER ITEM #2: (1) FOOD, TEMPLES, AND YOUNG BELIEVERS

1 Corinthians 8:1–13

¹ *Now about food sacrificed to idols: We know that "We all possess knowledge." But knowledge puffs up while love builds up.* ² *Those who think they know something do not yet know as they ought to know.* ³ *But whoever loves God is known by God.*

⁴ *So then, about eating food sacrificed to idols: We know that "An idol is nothing at all in the world" and that "There is no God but one."* ⁵ *For even if there are so-called gods, whether in heaven or on earth (as indeed there are many "gods" and many "lords"),* ⁶ *yet for us there is but one God, the Father, from whom all things came and for whom we live; and there is but one Lord, Jesus Christ, through whom all things came and through whom we live.*

⁷ *But not everyone possesses this knowledge. Some people are still so accustomed to idols that when they eat sacrificial food they think of it as having been sacrificed to a god, and since their conscience is weak, it is defiled.* ⁸ *But food does not bring us near to God; we are no worse if we do not eat, and no better if we do.*

⁹ *Be careful, however, that the exercise of your rights does not become a stumbling block to the weak.* ¹⁰ *For if someone with a weak*

conscience sees you, with all your knowledge, eating in an idol's temple, won't that person be emboldened to eat what is sacrificed to idols? [11] So this weak brother or sister, for whom Christ died, is destroyed by your knowledge. [12] When you sin against them in this way and wound their weak conscience, you sin against Christ. [13] Therefore, if what I eat causes my brother or sister to fall into sin, I will never eat meat again, so that I will not cause them to fall.

I once read about a pastor who said he loved pastoring most when he could go to the church when no one was there! We can cut the man some slack because he loved to open the doors and enter the sanctuary in the early hours of the day for his private worship. But there's something nonetheless humorous about the statement. What is a church without people? Not a church. The church *is* the people, building or not. Living together means living with people who don't get along. That's what church life is all about.

Now to the Corinthian church: the problem in that church, as in our churches today, was the people! Someone always had a complaint, was into some mischief, committing some egregious sin, or failing to see that the religions of Rome and faith in Jesus Christ were utterly incompatible. The impact of problem people in a church is felt by those most in need of pastoral care. Anyone who has encountered divisive cliques in a church will know those most wounded, offended, even scandalized are those in need of pastoral care.

Speaking of the problem people in that church in Corinth . . . people like to measure themselves over against others. Often, the standard for measurement is enlightenment, which in 1 Corinthians is one of Paul's most-used terms: knowledge (*gnosis*).* The "enlightened" strut their knowledge, spout out a few slogans that unite them, look down on the

---

* Nine times in 1 Corinthians; six times in 2 Corinthians.

unenlightened, and can even form into a theological clique, though it is not clear how widespread the problem in today's reading is. As happens in nearly every chapter in this letter to the Corinthians, we can learn from Paul's approaches to people problems in the church. In today's chapter, we can learn to become more sensitive to maturing believers, and we can also learn to be on the lookout for older, more confident believers to constrain their confidence.

WHAT WAS GOING ON
IN CORINTH?

The second item raised in the letter sent to Paul from Corinth gets a lengthy response. From 8:1 through 11:1 Paul addresses the toxic combination of food, temples, and phantom-gods or demons. Today's reading opens with "Now about food sacrificed to idols" (8:1). The words "food sacrificed to idols" translates but one Greek work: *eidōlothutos*. That term is made of two words, *eidos* and *thuō*, the first meaning phantom, demon, religious idol. Paul connects these acts of worship to demons (10:20–21). The second means "sacrifice," which makes clear Paul's concern is that the Corinthian believers are participating in pagan temples and/or the emperor cult. Eating food at the temple or near the temple was one way of participating (8:4). The issue is not about purchasing previously sacrificed food now available in the local markets. It's deeper than what they eat. The issue is some kind of syncretistic worship, but for the Corinthians, it was civic religion. *How else to be a Corinthian?*, they may have asked Paul.

Topping this off is the recognition that only the high-status and wealthy Corinthians get invited to these temple festivities. Their so-called knowledge "puffs up" or "enhances status" (8:1; *Second Testament*). The status claims for many in

Corinth had become a significant problem that led to cliques (4:6, 18–19; 5:2). The major division in today's passage was between those with status and the poor. In fact, as Jaime Clark-Soles reminds us, "people with money eat meat and poor people eat grains" (Clark-Soles, *1 Corinthians*, 40). Paul uses the word for "meat" in the last verse in today's reading.* In Corinth, a market was adjacent to the huge Temple of Apollo, which was kitty-corner to two more temples. Not to go to the temples meant one was not a true Roman or Corinthian; to go to the temples meant one was Roman. It was not possible to be a consistent Christian and worship both the one God and the gods of Rome.

SLOGANS OF ENLIGHTENMENT

The NIV again suggests Paul quotes a slogan when it puts quotation marks around "We all possess knowledge" (8:1). The "We all" reminds us that it is not knowledge but what we do with it. There are as many as five such slogans in today's passage. These slogans are probably the words of some high-status believers in Corinth, but Paul can at times identify with what they believe. The NIV does not put all of these slogans in italics. Other specialists in 1 Corinthians do.

1. "We all possess knowledge."
2. "An idol is nothing at all in the world" (8:4).
3. "There is no God but one" (8:4).
4. "But food does not bring us near to God" (8:8).
5. "We are no worse if we do not eat, and no better if we do" (8:8).

---

* For the Jewish Paul, the word "meat" (8:13), in Greek *krea*, almost certainly has the sense of defiled food (hence, *treif* for the observant).

What did these folks think? If we add up all five of these proposed slogans, this is what they were doing: they were going to Corinth's temples, they were participating in the religious activities there, they were participating in the cult meals, they brought home food offered to phantom-gods, and—here's the kicker—*they didn't think it mattered one bit because their super-knowledge permitted them to transcend the religious practices.* A kind of *since the idols are phantoms, it doesn't matter.* For Paul, what they were doing mattered, and what mattered was the impact of this "knowledge" in the assemblies in Corinth. In chapter ten, Paul will make it clear eating food sacrificed to idols can be done in certain situations (cf. 10:23–11:1).

TRUE ENLIGHTENMENT

What matters most is love: the claim to enlightenment degraded the status of others. Paul counters status-formation with inner-formation. That is, "love builds up," with building up directing attention to the formation of Spirit-based character, relations, and gifts (8:1). Riffing on the claim to knowledge, Paul contends these high-status folks only "think" they have true knowledge. He uses two parallel conditional sentences, and I quote from *The Second Testament*, which provides a very literal reading of 8:2.

> *If* it looks like someone has known something, that
> person did not yet know it is necessary to know.
> *If* someone loves God, that person has been known
> by him [God].*

---

* Both the ESV and CEB have these conditional sentences; the NIV and NRSVue use "Those who" or "Anyone who."

Spirit-formed knowledge—slow down to catch this with both hands—is love for God, and such an intimate love for God leads to being "known *by* God" (8:3). Paul counters a status claim to knowledge with loving God. And loving God *is* knowledge!

A love-shaped knowledge of God, which begins with God love-knowing us, leads to knowing God through the Spirit as the "one God, the Father" who is the creator of all and the direction of the one true life, and as the "one Lord, Jesus Christ" who likewise is the creator of all and "through whom we live" the one true life (8:4–6; notice how this reshapes the famous Shema of Deuteronomy 6:4–5). They all believe this about God. But *what* they know can be defeated by *what they do with it*. For Paul there is knowledge and there is love-knowledge. Love-knowledge leads not to status-mongering or to compromised worship but to pastoral care for others. The deepest knowledge is love. As Tom Wright and Mike Bird say it so well, their "cheerful polytheism" required wholesale conversion to the one true God (Wright-Bird, *New Testament World*, 489).

CARING

The emphasis of this chapter shifts from Paul calling out the impact of the status consciousness on those Paul calls the "weak." The Corinthians ought to be more concerned with the weak. For some, their conversions out of temple sacrifices are not yet complete. Their "conscience," which is the inner working of one's moral judgments, is not yet robustly formed, is "weak" and will be "defiled" rather than cleansed (8:7). The issue, then, is not this food—food doesn't ultimately matter—but the pastoral care of others. Read the room and do what forms the community in being like Christ, that's what matters.

The NIV translates "your [pl.] rights" in 8:9, which evokes modern individualism in Western law, but the Greek term is best translated with "authority" (*exousia; Second Testament*). The status of some empowers them to impose their will on others, not least those being formed spiritually, and can lead the younger believers back into pagan religious practices. In fact, he fears their authority, and Paul's language suggests coercive "pounding" of their conscience (McKnight, *Second Testament*), to shape the lives of others can actually dissolve the young believer's faith (8:11–12). One gets the impression the status group was relentless in its defense of its practices.

All believers are so united in Christ that any offense against the weak is "sin against Christ" (8:12). Paul urges all to put down their defenses and learn the lesson of love-knowledge: not to do what causes a younger believer's faith to fall or fail. Sensitivity to those maturing into a more robust walk with Christ ought always to shape Christian conversations. The "weak" of 1 Corinthians ought not to become the appeal to those who are mature in the faith who want their view to obtain for the whole church. The weak in 1 Corinthians 8 are younger believers who need time for maturation.

And Paul will now turn to how he has learned the very principle of surrendering what he wants for the formation of community.

QUESTIONS FOR REFLECTION AND APPLICATION

1. How does some Corinthians' sense of superior knowledge contribute to the issues Paul is addressing with them?

2. What does love-knowledge lead to, in Paul's view?

3. How does Paul want conscience-formation to factor into the believers' choices?

4. Do you see any practices of syncretistic worship in churches today?

5. How do you see matters of conscience being handled in the church today in ways that could harm the "weak"?

LETTER ITEM #2:
(2) FOOD, TEMPLES,
AND PAUL'S EXAMPLE

1 Corinthians 9:1–27

The Apostle's Authorization

¹ *Am I not free? Am I not an apostle? Have I not seen Jesus our Lord? Are you not the result of my work in the Lord?* ² *Even though I may not be an apostle to others, surely I am to you! For you are the seal of my apostleship in the Lord.*

³ *This is my defense to those who sit in judgment on me.* ⁴ *Don't we have the right to food and drink?* ⁵ *Don't we have the right to take a believing wife along with us, as do the other apostles and the Lord's brothers and Cephas?* ⁶ *Or is it only I and Barnabas who lack the right to not work for a living?*

⁷ *Who serves as a soldier at his own expense? Who plants a vineyard and does not eat its grapes? Who tends a flock and does not drink the milk?* ⁸ *Do I say this merely on human authority? Doesn't the Law say the same thing?* ⁹ *For it is written in the Law of Moses: "Do not muzzle an ox while it is treading out the grain." Is it about oxen that God is concerned?* ¹⁰ *Surely he says this for us, doesn't he? Yes, this was written for us, because whoever plows*

and threshes should be able to do so in the hope of sharing in the harvest. ¹¹ If we have sown spiritual seed among you, is it too much if we reap a material harvest from you? ¹² If others have this right of support from you, shouldn't we have it all the more?

But we did not use this right. On the contrary, we put up with anything rather than hinder the gospel of Christ.

¹³ Don't you know that those who serve in the temple get their food from the temple, and that those who serve at the altar share in what is offered on the altar? ¹⁴ In the same way, the Lord has commanded that those who preach the gospel should receive their living from the gospel.

The Apostle's Decision

¹⁵ But I have not used any of these rights. And I am not writing this in the hope that you will do such things for me, for I would rather die than allow anyone to deprive me of this boast. ¹⁶ For when I preach the gospel, I cannot boast, since I am compelled to preach. Woe to me if I do not preach the gospel! ¹⁷ If I preach voluntarily, I have a reward; if not voluntarily, I am simply discharging the trust committed to me. ¹⁸ What then is my reward? Just this: that in preaching the gospel I may offer it free of charge, and so not make full use of my rights as a preacher of the gospel.

The Apostle's Strategy

¹⁹ Though I am free and belong to no one, I have made myself a slave to everyone, to win as many as possible. ²⁰ To the Jews I became like a Jew, to win the Jews. To those under the law I became like one under the law (though I myself am not under the law), so as to win those under the law. ²¹ To those not having the law I became like one not having the law (though I am not free from God's law but am under Christ's law), so as to win those not having the law. ²² To the weak I became weak, to win the weak. I have become

all things to all people so that by all possible means I might save some. [23] I do all this for the sake of the gospel, that I may share in its blessings.

The Apostle's Goal

[24] Do you not know that in a race all the runners run, but only one gets the prize? Run in such a way as to get the prize. [25] Everyone who competes in the games goes into strict training. They do it to get a crown that will not last, but we do it to get a crown that will last forever. [26] Therefore I do not run like someone running aimlessly; I do not fight like a boxer beating the air. [27] No, I strike a blow to my body and make it my slave so that after I have preached to others, I myself will not be disqualified for the prize.

The best form of education is to observe an expert and then attempt what has been learned with the expert mentoring. My father taught me how to mow the lawn. His first lesson was to mow a straight line by concentrating my eyes on the far end and to mow straight toward that spot. I was taught not to look to the left or to the right or even down at the mower or grass as the line would then become crooked. More than sixty years later, I always begin mowing our grass by finding a specific spot at the end of the lawn to form a straight line. I'm proud to say the lines left by the mower's wheels reveal doggone straight rows.

In today's passage, Paul uses himself as an example of the "straight line" of denying what he wants in order to be of service to others. Jaime Clark-Soles says the chapter is "Paul models . . . what it looks like to set aside the self-centered ego and use one's power/status/liberty . . . for others to lead them into wholeness and healing" (Clark-Soles, *1 Corinthians*, 47). The last verse of the larger section of Letter Item #2 confirms how to read chapter nine: "Follow my example, as I follow the example of Christ" (11:1). Chapter nine defines the meaning of "example." The entire chapter instructs the Corinthian high-status believers to surrender their wills to the growth of younger believers. The apostle Paul rarely discloses, unlike most of us these days, his heart and soul so clearly. It appears the Corinthians drew Paul out of himself. The chapter in some ways discloses the mission strategy of the apostle Paul.

AUTHORIZATION: PROVISIONS

The NIV translation opens with Paul pressing the Corinthians to answer four questions. One about his freedom, one about his apostolic status, one about having seen the Lord Jesus himself, and one about the Corinthian believers owing their faith to the ministry of the apostle (9:1–2). Freedom is the implication of being sent (meaning of "apostle") by Jesus on his gentile mission. The freedom of which he speaks is freedom to be supported with "food and drink," one's wife's accompaniment, housing, coworkers, and funds when needed—by the Corinthians (9:3). In other words, "to not work" (9:6). Paul goes on the "defense" because he's being accused (see Introduction, pp. 1–16). He doesn't spell out the accusations, but we do know he was accused, and this may surprise you, of *not accepting donations from them.* The Corinthians were offended by Paul snubbing their offers. Paul did not accept funds from church plants until that church had become more stable and the believers more mature. His policy aggravated them even more.

One idea Paul appeals to is freedom, but he repeats in the NIV the idea of rights no fewer than six times (9:4, 5, 6, 12, 15, 18). Yet, again, the idea of "rights" can easily distract us into our constitutional rights—and that's not at all what Paul has in mind. The Greek term is *exousia*, which has the sense of authorization (by someone with authority) to receive something. The Lord Jesus' commissioning of Paul, not to ignore the Lord's brothers, Cephas, or Barnabas (9:5, 6), authorized apostles to go about their ministry without having to work manually because the churches would provide for their ministers. Such authorization, or his "right," corresponds to a soldier, a vintner, a shepherd, a farmer, and the Law itself (9:7–10). From each, we learn the worker deserves pay for the work. Paul transfers these examples from the physical work level to the spiritual work level to say the latter deserves provisions as well (9:11). His conclusion, which he offers only to proceed to two more proofs for his point, is that he has the authority, as others do, to be supported (9:12). One could guess Peter and Apollos had received material support from the Corinthians. He adds two more proofs: first, those who serve in the (Jerusalem's) temple get their provisions from their spiritual labor; second, Jesus ordered that "those who preach the gospel should receive their living from the gospel" (9:14).

Press release from Paul: I have the authority to use my authority. I have been authorized as an apostle by Jesus, and apostles deserve to be provided for on the basis of their ministry. For Paul, the legitimacy of his authority and the use of his authority jarred one another for power. The powers at work in the authority structures of his day, which were visible among the Corinthians at times, conflicted with the way Jesus wanted Paul to use his authority. He chose the way of the cross instead of the way of Rome. The way Paul used his authority, so unlike the divisionists of Corinth, was to subvert authority by flipping it upside down into self-denial. He used his "authority over" as an "authority for" the formation of others.

DECISION: SELF-DENIAL

The irony of Paul's eye-to-eye argument from verse one to verse twelve, and then from verse thirteen to fourteen, meets an unmovable stiff arm to the Corinthians' chest: "But we [Paul and Barnabas] did not use this right" and "But I have not used any of these rights" (9:12, 15). Okay, you ask, *why go to such lengths to make the point?*

Good question. Surely more than one person in a house church asked that very question to the one reading this letter to them. First, he did not prove that he should be paid "in the hope that you will do such things for me" (9:15). Second, he wants to boast (in a good Greek, Roman manner) of his independence. Third, he can boast about his gospeling "voluntarily"—that is, "on my own" (9:17; *Second Testament*). He wants to preach "free of charge" in order to acquire a completely different "reward" (see in 9:24–27). And he does not want to "make full use of my rights as a preacher of the gospel" (9:18)—and here we get the main point of Paul the example. He has surrendered his rights, his authorization, his freedom, and his desires for one reason and one reason only: to preach the gospel *free of social entrapments*.

He wants the Corinthian upper set to deny their rights and wishes, to deny themselves for the good of the weak in Corinth who need time to grow in spiritual maturity. This is what Jaime Clark-Soles over and over calls the "Logic of Love," which is the "Logic of the Cross" (Clark-Soles, *1 Corinthians*, 18, 39). His choice countered the wishes of the high-status Corinthians, and that makes his choice an act of resistance. A resistance that communicated not *Romanitas*, but the way of Christ. Out of love, out of the logic of following the Jesus of the cross, Paul chooses not to receive provisions.

For a reason. His strategy.

STRATEGY: REDEMPTION FOR ALL

Paul's mission strategy folds into a paradox: "being liberated from all, I enslaved myself to all" (9:19; *Second Testament*).* The "all" to whom Paul has enslaved himself includes "Jews" and "those under the law" and "those not having the law" and the "weak" (9:20–22). That is, he has used his agency to surrender his desires for the sake of the gospel mission to "all people so that by all possible means I might save some." He repeats with "I do all this for the sake of the gospel" and then takes the next step, which he develops in our next section, "that I may share in its blessings" (9:22–23). "All things to all people" was Paul's missionary strategy. All day long. Wherever he was. Whomever he was with.

This does not mean Paul can do whatever he likes. Paul constrains his behaviors, in self-denial, in alliance with his gospel's mission to reach anyone and everyone, wherever they are. His adaptability and flexibility may have offended others, but Paul sought to use these categories as his guiding lights.

Gordon Fee wonders if Paul would not have been accused in these few verses of being "chameleonlike" (Fee, *First Corinthians*, 467). Apparently, when he was, say, in Jerusalem or amongst observant Jews, Paul was observant; when he was with gentiles ("those not having the law") he did not insist on observance. I don't know if Paul discovered the succulence of ham or shellfish when he was in Ephesus or Corinth. What I do know is that his critics accused him of too much and too often. The intent of Paul's accommodating, adapting mission strategy was to "win" or to gain a gospel advantage with them (9:19, 20, 21, 22). His idea of winning

---

* The NIV's addition of "and belong to no one" is an expansive paraphrase of, translating literally, "from all" (9:19; *ek pantōn*).

was "that I might *save* some" (9:22). His strategy was not chameleon-ish but simple (and very Jewish) accommodation to circumstances. Not just to fit in. No, Paul fit in to reach others with the gospel.

GOAL: GOD'S FINAL APPROVAL

When Paul closed down verse twenty-three with "blessings," that word must have set his mind into wondering about his final destiny. As he used "win" several times only to clarify it with "save" in the previous passage, so in this last passage, Paul uses "prize" and "crown" in a way that turns each of those terms into the spiritual, eternal destiny of those in Christ. Normal human realities, especially the well-known Isthmian Games in Corinth, provide for Paul some metaphors: runners in a race, competitors in "strict training," and a "boxer" provide images of the goal. Their goal is to win, and Paul's goal is the blessing of an eternal crown (9:24–27).

What becomes exemplary from Paul's own strategy and practices is his self-discipline: "I pound my body and enslave [it]" (9:27; *Second Testament*). The images are all over the internet, and many of us see folks working out daily—mostly to enhance health. Some, however, are training for an event so they can do their best. I grew up with a father who was a coach. Rigorous practices, weightlifting, and preparation were common subjects of conversation. Paul seems to have been at least aware of the competitive games held in cities like Corinth. For him, those games became metaphors of the apostle's attempts to be a good example for those willing to sacrifice their desires for the liberation and maturation of others.

QUESTIONS FOR REFLECTION
AND APPLICATION

1. Often, people get irritated with Christian leaders for asking for money, but the Corinthians were irritated with Paul for *not* accepting money from them! What do you make of that situation?

2. How does Paul subvert the Corinthians' expectations of authority?

3. What point does Paul want to make in his example of refusing the provisions that he could demand as an apostle?

4. How did Paul's cultural adaptation work toward a gospel purpose?

5. In what ways could you give up your rights or privileges in order to better preach the gospel to others?

LETTER ITEM #2:
(3) FOOD, TEMPLES,
AND TYPES

1 Corinthians 10:1–22

^{1} For I do not want you to be ignorant of the fact, brothers and sisters, that our ancestors were all under the cloud and that they all passed through the sea. ^{2} They were all baptized into Moses in the cloud and in the sea. ^{3} They all ate the same spiritual food ^{4} and drank the same spiritual drink; for they drank from the spiritual rock that accompanied them, and that rock was Christ. ^{5} Nevertheless, God was not pleased with most of them; their bodies were scattered in the wilderness.

^{6} Now these things occurred as examples to keep us from setting our hearts on evil things as they did. ^{7} Do not be idolaters, as some of them were; as it is written: "The people sat down to eat and drink and got up to indulge in revelry." ^{8} We should not commit sexual immorality, as some of them did—and in one day twenty-three thousand of them died. ^{9} We should not test Christ, as some of them did—and were killed by snakes. ^{10} And do not grumble, as some of them did—and were killed by the destroying angel.

^{11} These things happened to them as examples and were written down as warnings for us, on whom the culmination of the ages has *come. [12] So, if you think you are standing firm, be careful that you don't fall! [13] No temptation has overtaken you except what is common to mankind. And God is faithful; he will not let you be tempted beyond what you can bear. But when you are tempted, he will also provide a way out so that you can endure it.*

[14] Therefore, my dear friends, flee from idolatry. [15] I speak to sensible people; judge for yourselves what I say. [16] Is not the cup of thanksgiving for which we give thanks a participation in the blood of Christ? And is not the bread that we break a participation in the body of Christ? [17] Because there is one loaf, we, who are many, are one body, for we all share the one loaf.

[18] Consider the people of Israel: Do not those who eat the sacrifices participate in the altar? [19] Do I mean then that food sacrificed to an idol is anything, or that an idol is anything? [20] No, but the sacrifices of pagans are offered to demons, not to God, and I do not want you to be participants with demons. [21] You cannot drink the cup of the Lord and the cup of demons too; you cannot have a part in both the Lord's table and the table of demons. [22] Are we trying to arouse the Lord's jealousy? Are we stronger than he?

When I was learning Greek in college, our textbook had a little saying we were asked to put to memory in Greek: *meletē to pan.* Repetition, or practice, is everything. The saying is attributed, it so happens, to an ancient ruler of Corinth (Periander). Our Greek teacher reminded us that only if we practiced our Greek daily would we learn the language well. The Greek word *meletē* was used at times for military drills in the development of skills. So, I like the translation that uses the term "repetition." What Paul repeated so often that it penetrated into his bones were the stories of Israelites in his scriptures. His ancestors were life and love for him. He knew them as uncles and aunts and sisters and brothers. Many think he had the whole of our Old Testament memorized. And so much was he committed to serving gentiles the gospel that his quotations of the Old Testament nearly always are citations from the Greek translation.

Remembering Scripture's teachings, stories, and characters both instructs us and becomes a fertile source for pondering new situations. Here the apostle Paul demonstrates how Scripture memory enabled him to instruct the Corinthians on how to respond to the system of worship they inherited from Rome and their ancestors. Conversion to Jesus required them to expand their ancestors from the world of Rome and Greece to Judea and Jewish history. Which is why Paul begins today's reading with "I do not want you to be ignorant" or, as in *The Second Testament*, "uninformed" (because some probably were; 10:1). Paul now informs them of their new story, a story that could help them live together in unity.

REMEMBERING OUR ANCESTORS

The spiritual ancestors of the Corinthians were slaves in Egypt, were liberated by the mighty hand of God under the leadership of Moses and Aaron, and were guided by the cloud and pillar of fire. The journey to the Land began when they were "all baptized into Moses." They were sustained by the "same spiritual food" (manna) and "drank from the spiritual rock," which Paul interprets as "Christ" himself (10:1–4). They are an example of salvation, of divine guidance, and of a gifted pastoral leader.

We need to skip down in our passage to verse eighteen to remember one more element of Israel's story: "Look at *Yisraēl* [Israel] consistent with the flesh: Are not the ones eating the sacrifice sharing a common life with the sacrificial altar?" (McKnight, *Second Testament*). A major moment here: the act of participating in temple worship in Jerusalem, all

Israelites know, joins the worshiper with the priests, the law, the nation, and the Land. They enter into a "common life," or they "participate" (NIV).

PERCEIVING TYPES

The Israelites both knew redemption and, in the mobile temple called the "tabernacle," they learned to participate in the work of God. But they failed the basics of faithfulness. "God was not pleased with most of them." Many died in the wilderness before entering the Land. Their failure now becomes an example for the Corinthians. That is, their new ancestors are "examples" or, better yet, "types" for them to consider, but they are not good types. A type is more than a moral example. A type is a pattern deserving pondering, cogitating, and exploring in the imagination. Types embody the faith or denial of the faith. Major types on Israel's story include the exodus, which is a type of God's liberating redemption; crossing the Red Sea, the wilderness temptations, the rock with a spring of water, the cloud, manna and quail, Mount Sinai, crossing the Jordan River, and not to be forgotten is apostasy. Each of these are explored in various ways by the authors of the New Testament. Paul makes one more than clear: he calls the Red Sea experience a baptism (10:2).

The Israelites' behaviors in the wilderness revealed to the Corinthians how not to set their "hearts on evil things" (10:6). The ancient Israelites' sin was idolatry, which alarmingly followed immediately after worshiping an idol, and evidently their "revelry" involved "sexual immorality" (10:7–8) The very sin Paul observes happening in Corinth (again, 8:1–13). Their sins included idolatry, revelry, sexual immorality, provoking God, and constant grumbling about how good it was in Egypt and how bad it was in the wilderness

(10:6–10). These sins are reported in Numbers 25:1–9; 21:5–9; 14:1–38. Each of these sins led to divine judgment, and we are perhaps to see these as anticipations of the weaknesses, sicknesses, and deaths mentioned in 11:30–31.

Since Paul used negative types, we need to consider the same. We need to pause long enough to ponder and perceive the sins of our world. I teach in a seminary where warnings about the abundance of pastoral failures need to be heard. My daughter and I have written two books that describe both the power abuses and sexual abuses of pastors and churches, and we have offered elements as well that can nurture a good culture in churches (McKnight, Barringer, *A Church Called Tov*; *Pivot*). Churches today are increasingly facing a crisis over marriages and divorces, examples abound of the latter, but they are in need of both good examples and more concentrated teachings about love, about marriage, about mutual respect, about boundaries, about intimate partner violence, and about parenting. Churches today have failed to offer solid teaching on what should be called "political discipleship," namely, calling believers to living under Jesus as Lord and not falling for the idolatry of political power (McKnight-Matchett, *Revelation for the Rest of Us*). Churches have failed to embody racial reconciliation and have collapsed far too often into complicity in systemic racism (Tisby, *The Color of Compromise*; *How to Fight Racism*). So, let's not point a long finger at either ancient Israel or Corinth when we've got these sins lurking in our churches. And we could name names and other sins.

COMPLICATING COMPLICITY

So, Paul calls them to leave the sins of idolatry, revelry, sexual immorality, provoking God, and constant grumbling. He would be calling us to abandon racism and its systemic pervasiveness, to repent and lament, and to repair our society by forming systemic equality, transparency, safety, peace, and justice. To abandon power and sexual abuses by leaders, to find pastors with good character and a consistent example, regardless of how great they are on the platform. In fact, Paul would have sharp words about even thinking of platforms. He'd call us to abandon sexism as he walks away from the movie *Barbie* with friends to discuss the insidious problems of patriarchy. He would call us to think far more deeply about capitalism and greed and the American thirst for more and more of what matters less and less.

The ancient Israelites were for the Corinthians exact examples of *how not to live faithfully*. From their examples, the Corinthians were to learn faithfulness. Paul told them "be careful that you don't fall" as they did (10:12). In fact, he knows the powers of temptation. He knows that what they and we all face is (1) all so "human-like" (McKnight, *Second Testament*), (2) that God is altogether faithful and there for us in our temptations, and (3) that God will therefore not permit us to enter any situation that we can't escape. We are to observe that Paul puts the agency for falling for temptations on our shoulders. He knows God is faithful, and so did the Reverend Gardner C. Taylor, when he preached these words:

> Do you think for a moment God would stand by and see his children beaten down and not step in? He loves and cherishes every moment of a soul toward him, toward godliness, toward holiness unto him, and he will not stand by and let us lose the battle. God is faithful! Say it to yourself when all hell rises against you. God is faithful! Repeat it when the hellhounds are baying on your trail, all earthly help has failed, and friends have walked away. God is faithful! Remember it when

dark clouds gather and strong winds blow. Whisper it in sickness and in sorrow. God is faithful! Let all the oppressed people everywhere know that the strength of the Almighty belongs to those of "low estate." (Taylor, *Words*, 108–109)

The theme of participation, or sharing a common life, matters in this passage, and a few more words need to be said. Paul's style of writing in some of these passages winds around and goes back and repeats what has been said and then switches lanes and jumps forward. In the eucharist, the "cup of thanksgiving," and the "bread that we break" are "common life with" the blood and the body of Jesus himself (10:15–16). That common life is shared by more than "me and God." The "one loaf" materially embodies the "one body" of Christ because we all share a common life in the eating and drinking (10:17).

With that message in our hearts, we need to hear his alarm over what's going on in Corinth. Those who share a common life with Christ's body and blood are drinking and eating bread at the pagan temples. "Any meal within sacred precincts or in a context that is dedicated to honoring one of the gods or goddesses is off limits" (Perkins, *First Corinthians*, 122). This is *spiritual adultery* for Paul—and that expression is very common to Israel's prophets. Paul lays down a heavy plank: "You cannot drink the cup of the Lord and the cup of demons too; you cannot have a part in both the Lord's table and the table of demons." And then he asks questions whose answers are obvious to all listening to the reading of this letter: "Are we trying to arouse the Lord's jealousy? Are we stronger than he?" (10:22). He evokes God's earlier judgments on the unfaithful (10:5, 8, 9, 10).

A word I want to complicate now is "complicity." Those who participate in eucharist are complicit in the ways of

Jesus, and those who participate in the sins of ancient Israel, the Corinthians, or our own American sins are complicit in the idolatry of drinking the cup of sin. We need to choose our complicity! Any complicity in the ways of sin wrecks our participation in the ways of Christ.

QUESTIONS FOR REFLECTION AND APPLICATION

1. Why does Paul tell the stories of Israel's people to the gentiles of Corinth?

2. How could the sins of the Israelites serve as warnings to the Corinthians?

3. How can the sins of the Israelites and the Corinthians serve as warnings to us in the church today?

4. What forms does "spiritual adultery" take in the church cultures near you?

5. In what areas of your life might you be complicit in the ways of sin? How can you become more complicit in the ways of Jesus?

FOR FURTHER READING

Scot McKnight, Laura Barringer, *A Church Called Tov: Forming a Goodness Culture that Resists Abuses of Power and Promotes Healing* (Carol Stream: Tyndale Momentum, 2020).

Scot McKnight, Laura Barringer, *Pivot: The Priorities, Practices, and Powers that Can Transform Your Church into a Tov Culture* (Carol Stream: Tyndale Momentum, 2020).

Scot McKnight, Cody Matchett, *Revelation for the Rest of Us: A Prophetic Call to Follow Jesus as a Dissident Disciple* (Grand Rapids: Zondervan Reflective, 2023).

Gardner C. Taylor, *The Words of Gardner C. Taylor, volume 3: Quintessential Classics* (Valley Forge: Judson, 2000).

Jemar Tisby, *The Color of Compromise: The Truth about the American Church's Complicity in Racism* (Grand Rapids: Zondervan Reflective, 2020).

Jemar Tisby, *How to Fight Racism: Courageous Christianity and the Journey Toward Racial Justice* (Grand Rapids: Zondervan Reflective, 2021).

LETTER ITEM #2: (4) FOOD, TEMPLES, AND SITUATIONS

1 Corinthians 10:23–11:1

[23] "I have the right to do anything," you say—but not everything is beneficial. "I have the right to do anything"—but not everything is constructive. [24] No one should seek their own good, but the good of others.

[25] Eat anything sold in the meat market without raising questions of conscience, [26] for, "The earth is the Lord's, and everything in it."

[27] If an unbeliever invites you to a meal and you want to go, eat whatever is put before you without raising questions of conscience. [28] But if someone says to you, "This has been offered in sacrifice," then do not eat it, both for the sake of the one who told you and for the sake of conscience. [29] I am referring to the other person's conscience, not yours. For why is my freedom being judged by another's conscience? [30] If I take part in the meal with thankfulness, why am I denounced because of something I thank God for?

[31] So whether you eat or drink or whatever you do, do it all for the glory of God. [32] Do not cause anyone to stumble, whether Jews, Greeks or the church of God—[33] even as I try to please everyone in

every way. For I am not seeking my own good but the good of many, so that they may be saved.

11:1 Follow my example, as I follow the example of Christ.

Situations matter. Decisions can be difficult. The path is not straight. The vision is murky. Yet we are called on to render a decision. Years ago, a student came into my office with a heavy heart accompanied by tears in her eyes. Her roommate was determined to get an abortion to hide her pregnancy from her pastor-father. The student looked me in the eye with a statement and questions for me: *She wants me to take her to the clinic for her abortion. Should I? Do you think I could persuade her not to at the last minute? Will I be complicit in her decision? How do I love my wonderful roommate in this situation?* Some decisions confronting us challenge us to the core of our moral being. Not because we don't have principles, but because the options enter into the borderlands between what is good and what is less than good. A medical doctor once told me, *I don't have a problem distinguishing between what is right and wrong. The problem is deciding between what is good and what is best.*

In today's passage, Paul reflects, like the trained rabbi he was, on situations and the appropriate response, but he also formulates no less than ten principles that can be turned into questions we can ask ourselves when rendering difficult decisions. For ease of reading, we turn to the situations and responses first. But you will notice as you read this passage that Paul riffs off the sheet music the way a skilled pianist can turn a few bars and lines into a two-minute adventure.

SITUATIONS AND RESPONSES

Paul was no newbie when it came to questions arising in gentile-shaped churches. Temples and idolatry were common concerns, as was then the sensitivity some had over meat that had been sacrificed in a temple, only later to be sold on the market.

Situation #1: Food sold in the market. Out of his mission work, Paul formulated a *general* approach for believers: "eat everything that is sold in the market" (10:25; *Second Testament*). And eat it "without raising questions of conscience," because God is the creator of all (10:25; NIV). The term "conscience" describes the capacity of a self-aware human to render conscious internal judgments. In verse twenty-nine Paul makes it clear he means one's consciousness of how others will evaluate one's decisions. Yet, as the next verses show, Paul's *general* approach doesn't determine the decision. Other common situations turn Situation #1 into two specific situations with differing decisions.

Situation #2: Food in an unbeliever's home. "If an unbeliever invites you to a meal . . . eat whatever is put before you." Paul adds "without raising questions of conscience," that is, without the invited one examining where the food came from (10:27). But . . .

Situation #3: Food previously sacrificed. If in someone's home the host informs the believer that the food before her or him has come from the temple markets, "then do not eat it." Two reasons: (1) for the sake of the person who informed you, who thinks you approve of both pagan and Christian worship, and (2) because of your consciousness of the host's judgment (10:28). It is not clear in Situation #3 if the host is a believer or an unbeliever, but I suspect the latter.

These three instructions from Paul jump straight into the middle of a complicated set of situations, discussions, decisions, debates, and practices. We get few details. What seems clear, though, is that Paul has concluded that the food in the market is acceptable for believers to eat because (1) there is no other God but one, but (2) each person needs to be sensitive to the impact of one's choices. But behind these three responses are a set of questions for us to ask.

PRINCIPLES AS QUESTIONS

In the following, I want to struggle through the principles Paul lays down. His principles are not sorted into tidy little moral buckets, and at times the principles themselves butt heads. But I will do my best to organize his principles into sorts. Perhaps a way to brace ourselves for the variety of principles appearing in this passage is what one essayist called "exceptions that prove no rules" (Epstein, *The Novel*, 107). As you read through our sorting out of Paul's principles, the essayist's "no rules" will be seen in our passage as no *inflexible* rules.

A MORALITY-BASED PRINCIPLE

Is it permissible? Paul opens today's passage with one bold claim repeated twice. The NIV again confuses things with the term "right" with "I have the right" (10:23). The term Paul uses is about what is permissible, what is allowable, and even what is possible. The term "right" is both too strong of a claim and too legal. For a Jew like Paul, one could translate with "it is observant," that is, it is in accordance with moral practices of the Pharisees. All three situations, and surely more could be added by the Corinthians, are permissible. That is, there is nothing against solid Christian teaching in eating food put before you.

OTHER-BASED PRINCIPLES

Paul chases and catches the permissibility question with a double response: I know it's permissible, but *is it beneficial or formative?* Then think of the impact of your decision on yourself and on the maturation of others. The other-consciousness so characteristic of the apostle's advice for churches has the capacity to create pastoral sensitivity and unity, but it also can be used by the abusive to manipulate and control.

The beneficial and formative questions are rooted in a wider question that can reshape our answers to morally difficult questions: *Am I being called to self-denial for the good of others?* Self-denial is neither self-punishment nor a denial of our safety, integrity, or significance, but choosing to surrender what we want for the good of others. Self-denial requires self-respect. These expressions clarify what Paul means in 10:24 with "No one should seek their own good, but the good of others." That is easy to misuse and abuse, even forming into self-abuse, if we don't bring in the other elements of self-care above. Some have been so neglected in their family of origin, have suffered at the hands of others, or have tirelessly, compulsively served others, that one more reminder of the need for self-denial spins down into a cycle of painful memories. At times, we are to say no to self in order to contribute to the formation of others, but this isn't complete self-abandonment.

The five uses of "conscience" in our passage prompt another question: *Do I need to respect the conscience of others?* Paul says in 10:29 that by "conscience" he is referring to the conscience of the unbelieving host and not the invited person. Of course, one can wonder how we know the conscience of another. They'd have to say something, that's how. There's a time to respect that conscience and there's a time when we may have to disagree as politely as possible.

A big principle Paul formulated in his mission churches was about the impact on others, leading in 10:32 to *Am I causing others to trip in their walk with Jesus?* This principle was found at 8:13 and he will raise it again in 2 Corinthians 11:29. Add to these Romans 14:13 and 16:17. The language is a picture of a person falling flat on their face or breaking a wrist in bracing the fall. Scandalizing another, at times a lame excuse, pertains to the immature believer slipping from or even out of the faith. Disagreements abound between Christians, and some can't handle disagreements. But scandalizing concerns immature believers and the impact of our decisions or behaviors on their walk with Jesus.

A final other-shaped principle for Paul flows into this question: *Will what I do lead to or block the salvation of others?* My fundamentalist upbringing liked to use a "no" answer to this question for why we teens were not to go to movies, not to go to school dances, not to smoke cigarettes, and not to drink alcohol. Let's hop lanes. The impact of our decisions on unbelievers matters immensely. We live in a self-serving society that bellyaches, resists, and even denounces this principle. At our own peril. If one believes in final redemption in Christ, as Paul did (and so do I), this question turns into a fork in our path.

SELF-SHAPED PRINCIPLES

The principles of Paul shift significantly in 10:29 when, thinking of the conscience of the other person, Paul forms another principle: *Am I not free?* You would not be the first to wonder how the principle that we are free to do as our conscience guides works with the principle of another's conscience. Paul maintains that he has the freedom to be judged alone by God and not by any other human.

This principle works along with another one he formulates immediately: *Am I giving thanks for the food I eat even if it comes from a sacrifice?* If so, Paul can return to what he said in 10:25: "eat anything sold in the meat market." He's free to do that, and he finds justification for eating in recognizing the food as God's gift to him. The emphasis here is on his own approach to the food: his giving thanks.

GOD-SHAPED PRINCIPLES

He legitimates his own decisions yet again with another principled question in 10:31: *Does what I do bring glory to God?* Eating, drinking, or doing whatever, the act can be brought before the principle of glorifying God. Otherness in making moral decisions here rises to the highest level: what matters is what God thinks and what brings glory to God. Which, once again, like other great ideas, is great as a principle until we come to a decision. (And others aren't so sure about our decision.)

Turn the pursuit of God's glory over and you get Paul's words in the last verse of today's passage: "Follow my example, as I follow the example of Christ" (11:1). The principled question would be *Is my behavior something Jesus would do?* Paul's terms matter here. I translate it, "Become copies of me just as I am of Christos" (McKnight, *Second Testament*). The deepest levels of formation find their roots in presence with someone worthy of copying or emulating or imitating. Moral maturity finds expression, not in a textbook or a set of laws, but in a person embodying the moral vision so clearly the person transcends the principle. Think Mr. Rogers. Think of those you know whom you would like to emulate. That's a God-shaped principle that can guide our decision-making.

Perhaps we ought to remind ourselves that no half chapter in the Bible covers all the grounds for making moral decisions, but we are not likely to find any chapter that covers more principles and situations than this one. Paul helps us think for ourselves by showing us how he thinks, and for that, we can be grateful. Charles Campbell entitles his section on today's passage "improvisational discipleship," and I like that very much (Campbell, *1 Corinthians*, 172–174). Paul's improvisations instruct us on ours.

QUESTIONS FOR REFLECTION
AND APPLICATION

1. Can you think of any current moral dilemmas that are similar to Paul's "food sacrificed to idols" dilemma?

2. What is the difference between permissible and beneficial?

3. Which of Paul's principles do you think is more important? Do you think they can be ranked?

4. Can you think of issues you feel the freedom of conscience to participate in but that might hurt the faith of weaker sisters and brothers?

5. If you were the student in the story, would you have taken your roommate to the clinic? Which of Paul's principles might inform your answer?

FOR FURTHER READING

Joseph Epstein, *The Novel, Who Needs It? An Essay* (New York: Encounter, 2023).

LETTER ITEM #3: WOMEN AND MEN IN WORSHIP

1 Corinthians 11:2–16

2 I praise you for remembering me in everything and for holding to the traditions just as I passed them on to you.

*[Paul] 3 But I want you to realize that
the head of every man is Christ,
and the head of the woman is man,
and the head of Christ is God.*

[Male opponents] 4 Every man who prays or prophesies with his head covered dishonors his head. 5 But every woman who prays or prophesies with her head uncovered dishonors her head—it is the same as having her head shaved.

[Paul] 6 For if a woman does not cover her head, she might as well have her hair cut off; but if it is a disgrace for a woman to have her hair cut off or her head shaved, then she should cover her head.

[Male opponents] [7] *A man ought not to cover his head, since he is the image and glory of God; but woman is the glory of man.* [8] *For man did not come from woman, but woman from man;* [9] *neither was man created for woman, but woman for man.* [10] *It is for this reason that a woman ought to have authority over her own head, because of the angels.*

[Paul] [11] *Nevertheless, in the Lord woman is not independent of man, nor is man independent of woman.* [12] *For as woman came from man, so also man is born of woman. But everything comes from God.*

[13] *Judge for yourselves:*
Is it proper for a woman to pray to God with her head uncovered?

[Male opponents] [14] *Does not the very nature of things teach you that if a man has long hair, it is a disgrace to him?*

[Paul] [15] *But that if a woman has long hair, it is her glory? For long hair is given to her as a covering.*

[16] *If anyone wants to be contentious about this, we have no other practice—nor do the churches of God.*

You will notice a (perhaps strange, perhaps a little unnerving) feature of today's reading. Alternative, opposing voices appear in the text. The ideas at work in today's reflection may seem unusual to you. It takes some familiarity to see this back-and-forth, but we are already accustomed, as is clear in the NIV, of putting some statements from the letter and report into quotation marks. Those statements were supposed quotations by Paul of those who had reported to him or who had asked questions in a letter. What is abundantly clear to those who study today's passage is that explaining the passage has become mind-boggling in disagreements, and many conflicting theories have been offered. Some statements in this passage, even the opening one in verse three attributed to Paul, do not sound like Paul. Nor do experts on 1 Corinthians agree about which words are Paul's and which are his opponents. Most do agree he is quoting others. I have edited the NIV above to show which words I think are best read as Paul's and which are the male opponents of Paul in Corinth.

BEGIN WITH THIS . . .

For more years than I care to count, today's passage has presented challenges for me. The problem revolved around the apparent *contradiction* between what is written in 11:7–10 when compared to 11:11–12. So, let's look at these verses first.

First, in 11:7–10 we read that man is (1) the image and glory of God, and that (2) man is also the glory *of* a woman. This suggests the men possess the image (and glory) of God in a way that women don't. I'd never seen anything like this in any other of Paul's letters. Then, second, we read man did not derive *from* woman but a woman *from* a man. And third, woman was created *for* the man. This of-and-from-and-for I also had not seen in Paul, but I could see how Paul may have been reworking Genesis 2. May have been. Now add that the enforcement of a veil or the long hair ideas in this passage all seem based on the male/female theology at work in 11:7–10.

Those three points from 11:7–10 are contradicted in the very next verses. These verses, as my friend Lucy Peppiatt has shown in several writings, reflect "the corrupted creation story of the Corinthians that was being used to keep women in a particular place in relation to men" (Peppiatt,

Rediscovering, 66). We read in 11:11–12 that "woman is not independent of man," which sounds a bit like 11:7–10, but then we read "nor is man independent of woman." That's a startling contrast with 11:7–10. They are *mutually interdependent upon one another,* which is not what vv. 7–10 teach, where the two are independent but with a woman dependent on a man. Now let's read on in verse twelve: "For as woman came from man, so also man is born of woman"! This, too, contradicts vv. 7–10, which teach not mutual interdependence, but independence and female dependence on a man. To smack down any chance of denying this mutuality, we read next this: "But everything comes from God" (11:12). Both men and women are dependent on God alone, and they are designed by this God for mutual interdependence with one another. What we read in 11:11–12 does not square with what we read in 11.7–10. They were not meant to square.

Paul constructs this passage for his listeners in Corinth to decide. Verse thirteen follows with this: "Judge for yourselves." You decide, he is saying, either they are independent in a hierarchy with men above women, that is, a patriarchy, or they are mutually interdependent and totally dependent upon God. The best explanation of this contradiction is that Paul is quoting someone in 11:7–10. The only other option is that Paul is hopelessly muddled, confused, and full of self-contradictions. He could not have gotten away with muddled thinking. Not with the Apollos-trained Corinthians, anyway. If you see this passage as I have just explained it, we can agree that in this passage Paul is going toe to toe with people in Corinth. Put in another way, not all in 11:2–16 is what Paul believes. It may not be easy to figure out what's from him and what's from his opponents, but we must try to disentangle them. If not, we end up with a flat contradiction in the span of six verses.

. . . AND WITH THIS TOO

Something similar happens in 11:13–15, and again I'm asking for your special patience with what is difficult to make clear. In 11:13a, Paul urges his listeners to "judge for yourselves." He wants them to decide. To make their decision, he asks two questions, and I want to suggest the first question is from Paul. (I will use *The Second Testament* because it is more literal.)

> Paul: "Is it appropriate for a woman to pray unveiled to God?"

He is asking that question because his opponents in Corinth think women ought to be veiled. Then I suggest he has the male opponents in Corinth come back with their particular ideas of the relationship about hair and hierarchy: "[Male opponents:] But doesn't nature itself teach you that a man, if he long-hairs it, is a dishonor to himself?" I doubt very much Paul buys this natural theology idea, so he comes back with his own question: "[Paul:] But if a woman long-hairs it, is it a splendor [or, glory] for her?" Notice that he uses the word "glory" for the woman by nature. Not because she's the glory of her man, as in 11:7! Which means he undercuts their uses of both glory and nature.

Undercutting gets more fierce with the end of verse fifteen. Paul overtly states that there is utterly no need for a veil because "her long hair is given to her instead of a covering [veil]." Put differently, the last line of verse fifteen completely undercuts the ideas at work in 11:14–15. Which leads me once again to think Paul is quoting someone else, because the ideas in verse fourteen and the question of verse fifteen don't fit Paul's own words at the end of fifteen. Complicated? I know. But there are so many tensions in these verses that an alternative explanation is needed.

THEN GO TO THE END

Nearly forty years ago, a former professor of mine (who was my colleague at the time) and I were in conversation when he heard I was vexed by today's passage, and he pulled me into his office. We sat down with our Greek texts, and he asked me to translate verse sixteen. So, I did, and it sounded very much like the NIV above. He looked at me and said, rather gently, *That translation is not accurate.* He proceeded to explain that the last verse ought to be translated something like this: "If someone looks to be argumentative [about what I have just proposed], we don't have *any such custom [about this], and neither do God's assemblies*" (11:16; *Second Testament*). The entire weight of this passage rests on what this verse means, and "we don't have any such custom" carries all its weight. The NIV has "we have no *other* practice" as if what Paul teaches in this passage is followed in all the churches. But the Greek word being translated, *toioutos*, does not mean "no other" but "any other." Big difference, eh? You bet. The NIV suggests all churches are doing this, and the other translation suggests that there are no fixed rules for the churches on long-hairing or short-hairing it in assemblies. Just to make it clear, the new *Cambridge Greek Lexicon* has this translation for our word: "such as this, of such kind, such." My colleague then said something like this. *Paul got done, threw up his arms, and said, "Do whatever you want."* He added a bit of color to that expression. I chuckled, he chuckled, and I went back to my office. Changed in how I read this passage. I have since studied it often and believe this translation is not only accurate, but that the NIV is mistaken.

This "we have no such custom" contrasts with what Paul writes to open today's reading. He honors the Corinthians "for holding to the traditions just as I passed them on to you" (11:2). Paul does not call what he writes in 11:3–15

153

a "tradition." His advice hasn't risen to the level even of a common custom (11:16). Our passage illustrates again Paul's wading into an internal issue at the church in Corinth, giving his conclusion, and then moving on. He does not lay down the law. He gives his opinion. He expects them to listen, and he'd like them to agree. He has no church custom or tradition to which he can appeal.

WHAT'S THE PROBLEM?

The problem in our passage has to do with the expectation, and perhaps even the requirement, that women "long-hair" it while men "short-hair" it (my translations). Along with required male and female hair length, some required that women wear a veil in the assemblies (11:4–7). Our proposed translation with voices above shows the clipped back-and-forth Paul creates as he responds. Some males in the church believed it was socially degrading for a man to wear a veil and degrading for a woman not to wear a veil (11:4–5). Male priests in Corinth wore a hood.

These same males in Corinth believed men were both the "image and glory" of God. The bit about glory is not found in Genesis 1–2. Women, these men believed without warrant from Genesis, were the glory of men (11:7).* Furthermore, they believed women came from men (Genesis has "rib" or "side"), not men from women (which counters every birth story since Genesis). They also believed women ought to have "authority" (NIV translated this term "right" at 9:3–6) on their heads, that is a veil visibly revealing their dependence on men. Now add some more: these men believed women were "created for man" (11:9). Two more arguments

---

* The NRSVue has "reflection" but the Greek word *doxa* does not mean "reflection" or even "reflected glory."

from these males are added: "because of the angels" (11:10) and "the very nature of things" (11:14). Swirl all this into the need to disentangle the voices, and we've got ourselves into a messy situation.

WHO'S THE PROBLEM?

The "what's the problem" question leads to a question with an answer that turns this passage upside down for some. As you can see from the previous section, the problem was not the women but the males. The men were demanding, or at least expecting, women to attire themselves according to what these men deemed consistent with their interpretation of Genesis. In the history of the church, many have argued that it was the women who were the problem. They were not the problem. Paul disagrees in this passage with males, not the women. The women, and this should not surprise us, have no voice here. The problem was the men.

PAUL NEXT TO HIS OPPONENTS

So, what is Paul's advice? In three separate instances Paul seems to be thinking along with the male opponents. But, in repeating their ideas, instead of agreeing with them totally, he extends their argument in a way that unravels their ideas. Notice the three observations in 11:3, where Paul affirms the head of the man is Christ, and the head of the woman is the man. But, very noticeably, he caps it all off with a potent reminder: "the head of Christ is God." He reminds of the same again in 11:12 with "But everything comes from God," and then in 15:28 with the Son subject to the Father "so that God may be all in all." Why does he do this? In a private communication, Lucy Peppiatt wrote me that "Paul dismantles and redefines the distorted 'headship' structures they've put in place . . . by reminding them they all have one head—God—from whom they are all derived" (email to me, 7.30.2023).

The male opponents' headship ideology used these three points of Paul's to push for women dressing according to the wishes of the men. Paul disagrees with their dress code, and that suggests that even these headship statements need to be seen as Paul running along with the Corinthian men in order to defeat them with a "the head of Christ is God."

At 11:6 he takes the males' argument that not wearing a veil is no different from being shaved, and Paul echoes that claim by rewording it: *If* it's degrading not to wear a veil, then women should just get shaved. He, of course, doesn't think they should get shaved or wear a veil. (Hair will do; see next paragraph.) To shave a woman's hair was to shame the woman. It has sometimes been argued that a shaved head characterized a prostitute. The evidence from Pompeii disproves the connection of shaved heads and prostitutes. The images we now know from Pompeii reveal prostitutes with stylish haircuts. One should perhaps, then, detect sarcasm or at least irony in what Paul writes in 11:6. He runs next to them to criticize their view.

And at 11:13 Paul asks if it is "inappropriate" for a woman to pray in the assembly "unveiled" (McKnight, *Second Testament*). (Paul thinks it is fine for a woman to pray unveiled. His opponents believe they should be veiled.) His question about what is inappropriate anticipates the very point the males in Corinth believe in 11:14. They have a nature argument: nature teaches men to short-hair it, with the implication that nature teaches women to long-hair it. Running alongside these Corinthian men with their argument from nature, Paul then takes their point to the next level by asking about a woman who prays with long hair, which she has by nature (right?)—is not her long hair glory?

(11:15). If that's the case, they don't even need a veil. They've got long hair!

Now what do we say at the end of this attempt to explain what is very difficult to explain? Paul was working pastorally with the Corinthians to get them to see that the men of Corinth were the problem. Their attempts to require women to dress in a specific manner may well have reflected their theology of creation, but Paul thought their theology was off base. His conclusion is that God made men and women in a mutually interdependent relationship, not a hierarchical or patriarchal relationship. That mutuality needs to be seen in their assemblies.

QUESTIONS FOR REFLECTION AND APPLICATION

1. What do you think of the arrangement of the verses as a disagreement between Paul and his opponents?

2. How does it change the meaning of the passage if verse 16 reads "any other custom" rather than "no other practice"?

3. Have you heard or read other interpretations of this passage? How does this explanation compare?

4. What changes for you if you consider that Paul didn't have a problem with the women in Corinth on this issue but with the men?

5. How could this teaching on mutuality impact practices around women and men in worship in your church?

FOR FURTHER READING

For her more accessible treatment, see Lucy Peppiatt, *Rediscovering Scripture's Vision for Women: Fresh Perspectives on Disputed Texts* (Downers Grove: IVP Academic, 2019). Her more academic study can be found at *Women and Worship at Corinth* (Eugene, Oregon: Cascade, 2015).

LETTER ITEM #4:
THE LORD'S SUPPER
AND SOCIAL STATUS

1 Corinthians 11:17–34

[17] In the following directives I have no praise for you, for your meetings do more harm than good. [18] In the first place, I hear that when you come together as a church, there are divisions among you, and to some extent I believe it. [19] No doubt there have to be differences among you to show which of you have God's approval. [20] So then, when you come together, it is not the Lord's Supper you eat, [21] for when you are eating, some of you go ahead with your own private suppers. As a result, one person remains hungry and another gets drunk. [22] Don't you have homes to eat and drink in? Or do you despise the church of God by humiliating those who have nothing? What shall I say to you? Shall I praise you? Certainly not in this matter!

[23] For I received from the Lord what I also passed on to you: The Lord Jesus, on the night he was betrayed, took bread, [24] and when he had given thanks, he broke it and said, "This is my body, which is for you; do this in remembrance of me." [25] In the same way, after supper he took the cup, saying, "This cup is the new covenant in my

blood; do this, whenever you drink it, in remembrance of me." [26] For whenever you eat this bread and drink this cup, you proclaim the Lord's death until he comes.

[27] So then, whoever eats the bread or drinks the cup of the Lord in an unworthy manner will be guilty of sinning against the body and blood of the Lord. [28] Everyone ought to examine themselves before they eat of the bread and drink from the cup. [29] For those who eat and drink without discerning the body of Christ eat and drink judgment on themselves. [30] That is why many among you are weak and sick, and a number of you have fallen asleep. [31] But if we were more discerning with regard to ourselves, we would not come under such judgment. [32] Nevertheless, when we are judged in this way by the Lord, we are being disciplined so that we will not be finally condemned with the world.

[33] So then, my brothers and sisters, when you gather to eat, you should all eat together. [34] Anyone who is hungry should eat something at home, so that when you meet together it may not result in judgment.

And when I come I will give further directions.

Paul's letters are never straight-up philosophy or systematic theology. His letters are written to specific people about specific problems among specific people. The letters are sent at specific times in his own life. His words are timely. His letters are situation-shaped. We can be grateful his timely letters are so timely for us, too.

The remembered tradition about the Lord's Supper was recorded in this specific letter because of a specific situation. Paul rehearses, or remembers, the Lord's Supper paragraph to counter the mistaken, unfortunate practices of the Corinthians. Our reflection will concentrate, then, on the use of this tradition by Paul for the problem in Corinth. So, we begin by looking again at a tragic situation.

THE SITUATION

Social status once again manifests itself in church gatherings. Two terms reveal the problem: (1) "divisions" or rips and tears in the fabric of the church and (2) "differences" or factions. Talk of divisions reminds us of chapters one through four. Paul turns these factions inside-out to render a strong judgment: they "show which of you have God's approval" (11:19). Their meals turn what should be a memorial meal into "not the Lord's Supper." This tragic conversion of a meal happens when the wealthy eat separate meals from the poor. The leisure of the wealthy allowed them to arrive early for drinks and a more up-scale meal, which would have involved meat, while the poor working believers arrived after their daily labor was over. The wealthy displayed at their meal a theater for other wealthy folks while the poor ate what was left over from the meals of the wealthy. Once again, Paul encounters a church divided as he strives for teaching them how to live together as God wants.

Ironically, I cannot imagine this happening at our churches, yet it happens in a different way. At times, the wealthy form supper clubs in spacious homes. They don't invite the poor, and the poor would not feel welcome. Since giving a banquet involves reciprocating by the invited, the poor cannot reciprocate, so they would not feel welcome because they could not reciprocate. Same thing but different.

Paul's opening words pound a loud drum: "you assemble not for the better but for the worse" (11:17; *Second Testament*). Today's passage about the practice of the Lord's Supper is famous in the church. But for this tragic social division in the assemblies in Corinth we would have heard it in Paul's words.

THE TRADITION

Without words of transition, Paul quotes from memory the tradition of the Last Supper found in the Synoptic Gospels (Mark 14:12–25; Matthew 26:17–29; Luke 22:7–38). In 1 Corinthians, Paul *uses* the tradition to denounce social status factionalism in Corinth. Paul clarifies his intent for remembering the tradition in 1 Corinthians 11:33–34, where he says in their gatherings they should "wait for one another" (*Second Testament*). The NIV paraphrases with "you should all eat together." The Lord's Supper ought to express an embodied unity of the whole assembly, and social status divisions ought to disappear entirely. The Lord's death, which they proclaim whenever they participate in the Lord's Supper, announces death to divisions and life to unity.

Their unity does not express mental or verbal agreement. Instead, they are united with Christ when they remember, and out of memory, eat the bread and drink the wine. They are remembering as they are ingesting the body and blood of Jesus himself. That cup, he says, is the "new covenant in my blood," which takes us back to Jeremiah 31:31–34. A line or two of Jeremiah echoes: "No longer will they teach their neighbor . . . because they will all know me, from the least of them to the greatest." That equality flows from God's forgiveness ("I will forgive their wickedness and will remember their sins no more" [31:34]). More than even echoing Jeremiah, our text takes us back to the Passover itself (Exodus 12). In the Passover God *liberated* the children of Israel from slavery. The meal memorializes liberation from all that shackles us. So, take your pick, he says to them, go back to Jeremiah or to Exodus.

Jesus offered himself to his disciples at the Last Supper. In our remembering, we hear the Lord offer himself to all of us. He offers to all of us the bread and the wine. We can all respond by taking and eating, taking and drinking. All we do is receive.

The Lord's Supper is, as Ellen Davis has said eloquently, "the event that enables us to make sense of everything else in our world" (Davis, *Preaching*, 288). This meal, the richness of it uncapturable in words and requiring eating and drinking truly to understand, embodies the gospel and the heart of the Christian faith. We turn in this meal to the death of Jesus on a cross, a brutal act against an innocent man, to turn the hideousness of systemic sins and injustices upside-down. We see in this death the meaning of life, and in life we perceive a death to sin and selfishness. In this death we see the love of God for all humans on full display. In this death we see what other-shaped love is all about. In God's love we see the "Logic of Love" (Clark-Soles, *1 Corinthians*, 63). In this death we see the sicknesses of divisiveness. All of this, and much more besides, can be extruded from why Paul went from factions to the tradition about the Lord's Supper.

THE DANGER

If we turn back a page or two in the Bible to chapter ten, verses one through ten, we read of God disciplining Israelites in the wilderness for their sins of sexual immorality and idolatry, even after experiencing God's redemption. So in today's reading, the social status divisions in Corinth meant their meals were not the Lord's Supper, regardless of their claims (11:20). They were eating "in an unworthy manner," or more tersely, "undeservingly" (McKnight, *Second Testament*) and so "sinning against the body and the blood of the Lord" (11:27). Paul hits repeat two verses later with "without discerning the body of Christ." That is, there was no boundary between their meals and the Lord's Supper. The two were fused into a late afternoon, early evening party.

Paul spares no words. Such irreverence leads to "judgment," to "discipline," to sicknesses, and even to death (11:29–32). Without repentance and correction, the Corinthians are indirectly warned with "that we will not be finally condemned with the world" (11:32). Paul offers some practices to replace this tragic display of power and status.

THE PRACTICES

Charles Campbell writes:

> The powers of this age use the theater of daily practices to reinforce the system of domination. Through such practices the system becomes normalized, taken for granted; it becomes the air we breathe. For this reason the church's practices are critical; the community of faith will not form imaginations or resist cultural accommodations simply by talking about alternatives or thinking about them; alternative practices are essential for resistance. (Campbell, *1 Corinthians*, 188, 192)

The practice of all eating at the same time, all eating together, all eating the same food—these practices undermine the social status systems of the world.

The corrections Paul offers involved three practices. The first is for each individual: each is to "examine" oneself, which I translate as "judge oneself suitable" (11:28). Just what "examine" meant is not crystal clear, but the sense is: pause, recollect, ponder, quiet the heart, slow down the mind, and become aware of your feelings. This self-introspection points to one's ability to judge if one is sufficiently conscious of what the Lord's Supper's elements mean. Why they are before us. What we do internally to take them in full participation of the grace of God that comes to us in the bread and wine. We concentrate. We discipline our attention away from those around us. We turn ourselves toward God in the face of Christ.

Yet, examining becomes corporate, too: "If we were more discerning with regard to ourselves" (11:31). The "we" and *our* in "ourselves" reveals this as an act of the community to end all satisfactions with status factions. Paul urges discrimination and we can do this by interrogation: Do our assemblies reflect social demographics or a pervasive unity in Christ?

Individuals need to ready themselves and so does the community. When these occur properly, the community sheds social division, waits for all to arrive, and then eats a family meal (11:33). He adds a little bit of wisdom, a kind of *If you're that hungry, eat something at home before you come.* Such wisdom suggests the purpose of the assembly was not a picnic or a meal, but a sacred meeting of the Lord in the Lord's Supper. That some were eating a meal mixed with the Lord's Supper before the poor could arrive blows apart the very purpose of the Lord's Supper.

SOME SUGGESTIONS

To be prepared for serious participation in the Lord's Supper, I recommend the following. The order does not matter. Pray about it. Discipline your mind and ears away from distractions. Read 1 Corinthians 11:23–26 or one of the passages mentioned above from the Synoptic Gospels. Or read a passage about Jesus, either from the Gospels or Philippians 2:6–11 or Colossians 1:15–20 or Revelation 5. Or read a passage about redemption, like Romans 3:21–26. Close your eyes. If music is playing, let that selected song guide your preparation. In weekly readings, read a good book about the Lord's Supper (see pp. 167).

Above all, turn all your thoughts to the essence of the Lord's Supper: God's deep and abiding love for us. As Ellen Davis put it, "the most risky *and* most loving thing that God has ever done is becoming flesh and blood in Jesus Christ—a supreme venture in love, which can end only in death" (Davis, *Luminous*, 289). David de Silva has a word for each of us when turning to the table. This meal is an "appetizer" of the banquet to come. Therefore, "we shouldn't be afraid to expect too much from Holy Communion, for this is a feast that has the potential *always* to exceed our expectations for it; we should be afraid to expect too little, lest we not prepare ourselves adequately for what God wishes to do in us and among us through it, lest we miss out because we weren't looking for it" (de Silva, *In Season and Out*, 154, 159).

QUESTIONS FOR REFLECTION AND APPLICATION

1. What was leading to the socially striated celebrations of the Lord's Supper, culturally speaking?

2. What practices does Paul offer to counter this problem?

3. If Jesus defeated sin and selfishness with his death, what should that have communicated to the Corinthians who were eating selfishly?

4. Where do socio-economic divides show up in your church community?

5. Which of the suggestions for preparing for the Lord's Supper might you want to adopt, and why?

FOR FURTHER READING

Ellen F. Davis, *Preaching the Luminous Word* (Grand Rapids: Wm. B. Eerdmans, 2016).

David A. de Silva, *In Season and Out* (Bellingham, Wash.: Lexham, 2019), 154.

Gordon T. Smith, *A Holy Meal* (Grand Rapids: Baker, 2005).

For the variety of views, the following two books are
recommended:

Understanding Four Views on the Lord's Supper
(Grand Rapids: Zondervan, 2007). The authors,
representing four different factions (!) of the
one church, are Russell D. Moore, I. John
Hesselink, David P. Scaer, Thomas A. Baima.

The Lord's Supper: Five Views (Downers Grove: IVP
Academic, 2008). The authors, representing
five more factions of the one church, are Jeffrey
Gros, John R. Stephenson, Leanne Van Dyk,
Roger E. Olson, Veli-Matti Kärkkäinen.

LETTER ITEM #5:
GIFTS OF THE SPIRIT
(1) GOD'S GIFTING

1 Corinthians 12:1–11

¹ Now about the gifts of the Spirit, brothers and sisters, I do not want you to be uninformed. ² You know that when you were pagans, somehow or other you were influenced and led astray to mute idols. ³ Therefore I want you to know that no one who is speaking by the Spirit of God says, "Jesus be cursed," and no one can say, "Jesus is Lord," except by the Holy Spirit.

⁴ There are different kinds of gifts, but the same Spirit distributes them. ⁵ There are different kinds of service, but the same Lord. ⁶ There are different kinds of working, but in all of them and in everyone it is the same God at work.

⁷ Now to each one the manifestation of the Spirit is given for the common good. ⁸ To one there is given through the Spirit a message of wisdom, to another a message of knowledge by means of the same Spirit, ⁹ to another faith by the same Spirit, to another gifts of healing by that one Spirit, ¹⁰ to another miraculous powers, to another prophecy, to another distinguishing between spirits, to another speaking in different kinds of tongues, and to still another the interpretation of tongues. [11] *All these are the work of one and the same Spirit, and he distributes them to each one, just as he determines.*

I was sheltered. I'm old enough to remember when spiritual gifts were both a new teaching in our sheltered churches and potentially dangerous. When the charismatic movement began to widen its influence, like a stone dropped straight down from heaven onto a waveless lake creating circled ripples, churches of our sort went on the defense. My youth pastor said those who spoke in tongues were demon-possessed. That was that. None dared to ask. We're talking late '60s and early '70s. In the '70s, many churches began to adopt and adapt the spiritual gift practices articulated by Ray Stedman in his book *Body Life*. By the '80s, the Vineyard movement had all but sanctified the legitimacy of the more "supernatural" of the gifts, like tongues, prophecy, and miracles. Tongue-speaking is oh-so ho-hum today.

If you are gobsmacked that pastors accused tongue-speakers of demon possession or that the era of miracles is over and that spiritual gifts are not for today, I hope to shout, to quote my father, that times have indeed changed. (We also didn't shout in our church.) Opposition to such gifts usually gets connected to the teaching called "cessationism," namely, that the more dramatic spiritual gifts have passed away while the common ones are here to stay. More than a few have observed that the ones that have stayed are the ones that teachers and preachers have, while those that have passed away have . . . well, you see the point. So unlike the days of Paul. People were competing with one another over the gifts, dramatic or not. Paul counters the competition by affirming God is the one who determines and grants the gifts.

Spirit People

The opening to today's reading in the NIV reads, "Now about gifts of the Spirit." But that's not quite right. Paul doesn't get to "gifts" until verse four. A more literal translation of 12:1 reads "Concerning the Spirit-[something]" or "Concerning spiritual [Spiritual] matters." Paul does not use the word "gifts" here. I believe it refers to persons, so in *The Second Testament* I translated "Concerning Spirit-(gifted)-persons." The verses that immediately follow are persons who either have the Spirit or don't. In their past the Corinthians did not. In their present they do. Those who don't have the Spirit curse Jesus. Those who do confess "Jesus is Lord." To confess Jesus truly as Lord cannot be done "except by the Holy Spirit" (12:3). So, perhaps we could translate "Concerning Spirit-prompted confessions"! Or maybe Paul's words are cheeky: "Concerning those who think they are ever-so-spiritual"!

God Gifts

From Spirit-speech Paul turns to the origins of all spiritual activities. God prompts all of it. There are differing sorts of gifts, kinds of service, and kinds of energies. But the *same* God inspires each: the same Spirit, the same Lord (Jesus), and the same God (the Father). On the edge of Paul's thinking later came to be Trinitarian theology. However you describe God's effective work in our world, and "gifts" is only one of the terms he uses, *God* is the one inspiring all of them. Notice how God works in our world: God grants what can be translated as *"grace-acts"* or even "moments of grace" (gifts [*charismata*] translates a term connected to God's grace [*charis*]). God empowers persons *to serve* others in this world, and God distributes through persons various forms of *energy* that empower people to do the work of God. My professor, James D.G. Dunn, once put it in a memorable expression: "for Luke the mission of the church could not hope to be effective without this empowering from God (the Spirit of God) which transcends human ability and transforms human inability" (Dunn, *Acts*, 12). Latch onto the ending of that sentence. It rocks. The Spirit gives the power to do what we otherwise could not do and takes what we can do and makes it better (and I'm not quoting Paul McCartney's "Hey Jude").

Each of these—grace-acts, service, energies—are "manifestations" of the Spirit of God. More importantly, each occurs through a person "for the common good" (12:7). The work of God in the Spirit does not intend to make any of us a celebrity, or a bestseller, or a pulpit sensation. We are but channels through whom the Spirit works for the formation of someone else. We are agents. We are not the gift or the giver of the gift. We receive and give away. Don't you think Paul had the divisive folks in mind when he wrote "for the common good"? (The opposite would have been "for ourselves.")

Each of us is an agent for God. Each of us can do something unique. Each of us contributes in different ways. Jaime Clark-Soles reminds us of what is known to many: "I am awestruck and dumbstruck when it comes to spiritual gifts. I'm awestruck by the brilliance and varieties of gifts that I see in people of all places and ages. I am dumbstruck by the number of people who (a) don't recognize their gifts or (b) don't understand the value of their gifts for the wider world" (Clark-Soles, *1 Corinthians*, 74). I would add a (c): some people would prefer that they had been given a different gift. Some would like to be the teacher or preacher in a church, in part because they think they have good ideas, but they don't have the gifting for it. Some would like to be a leader, but leadership is not their gift. (They want control.) Some just want to be on the platform or behind the pulpit, and they aren't gifted that way. Some who wanted to be in charge in Corinth created the divisions about which Paul is so concerned in this letter.

VARIED GIFTS

Now I register what remains important to me. There is no magical list, either here or at the end of chapter twelve, or in Ephesians 4 or in 1 Peter 4, or any list you and I could compose by adding all the gifts up. In today's passage, at verse seven, Paul calls all the gifts/services/energies a "manifestation of the Spirit." If we reverse the flow of that statement, we learn this: *anything the Spirit does through us for the good of another's Spirit-prompted formation is a gift/service/energy.* That includes singing a song in church, guiding a youth group, writing a blog post that touches folks, taking your kids to school or to camp, providing a flash of insight to another person . . . obviously I could go on. So could you. Embrace it. Whatever God uses you to do is a gift, even if only for that moment. Calling gifts something we "have" exceeds the teaching of the New Testament. We don't have gifts. We are used by God's Spirit to serve others. Being an instrument in the hands of God is not a possession of God!

Off that perch now.

Paul mentions a number of gifts/services/energies/manifestations. I count nine, and later in the chapter we get a different list (because there is no magical list). Sorry, I was back on the perch again. The gifts in today's passage are:

1. A word of wisdom
2. A word of knowledge
3. Faith
4. Curing
5. Energies of power

6. Prophecy
7. Distinguishing spirits
8. Tongues
9. Interpreting tongues

Each from God; each for others. God decides who becomes the instrument, or the moment of grace, for someone else. There is thus no reason to compete for gifts. We open ourselves to God's Spirit, and God does what only God can do.

Some of us have been wrecked and racked wondering which of the gifts we have. Let's completely junk the question "What is my gift?" to "What have I done to serve others?" That's your gift. God's working in you for the common good. Jaime Clark-Soles writes that one of her friend's gifts is being a "safe space" for others (Clark-Soles, *1 Corinthians*, 73). Don't you just love that?!

Be blessed.

QUESTIONS FOR REFLECTION AND APPLICATION

1. How are gifts linked to grace?

2. How do humans and God work together to bring gifts into the world?

3. What is the purpose of spiritual gifts?

4. Have you ever taken a spiritual gifts "inventory" or "test"? What gifts did it say you are gifted to use?

5. What have you done to serve others?

FOR FURTHER READING

James D.G. Dunn, *The Acts of the Apostles* (Grand Rapids: Wm. B. Eerdmans, 2016).
Ray Stedman, *Body Life* (Glendale, Calif., 1972).

LETTER ITEM #5:
GIFTS OF THE SPIRIT
(2) ONE BODY

1 Corinthians 12:12–31

¹² *Just as a body, though one, has many parts, but all its many parts form one body, so it is with Christ.* ¹³ *For we were all baptized by one Spirit so as to form one body—whether Jews or Gentiles, slave or free—and we were all given the one Spirit to drink.* ¹⁴ *Even so the body is not made up of one part but of many.*

¹⁵ *Now if the foot should say, "Because I am not a hand, I do not belong to the body," it would not for that reason stop being part of the body.* ¹⁶ *And if the ear should say, "Because I am not an eye, I do not belong to the body," it would not for that reason stop being part of the body.* ¹⁷ *If the whole body were an eye, where would the sense of hearing be? If the whole body were an ear, where would the sense of smell be?* ¹⁸ *But in fact God has placed the parts in the body, every one of them, just as he wanted them to be.* ¹⁹ *If they were all one part, where would the body be?* ²⁰ *As it is, there are many parts, but one body.*

²¹ *The eye cannot say to the hand, "I don't need you!" And the head cannot say to the feet, "I don't need you!"* ²² *On the contrary, those parts of the body that seem to be weaker are indispensable,*

²³ and the parts that we think are less honorable we treat with special honor. And the parts that are unpresentable are treated with special modesty, ²⁴ while our presentable parts need no special treatment. But God has put the body together, giving greater honor to the parts that lacked it, ²⁵ so that there should be no division in the body, but that its parts should have equal concern for each other. ²⁶ If one part suffers, every part suffers with it; if one part is honored, every part rejoices with it.

²⁷ Now you are the body of Christ, and each one of you is a part of it. ²⁸ And God has placed in the church first of all apostles, second prophets, third teachers, then miracles, then gifts of healing, of helping, of guidance, and of different kinds of tongues. ²⁹ Are all apostles? Are all prophets? Are all teachers? Do all work miracles? ³⁰ Do all have gifts of healing? Do all speak in tongues? Do all interpret?

³¹ Now eagerly desire the greater gifts.

And yet I will show you the most excellent way.

The Spirit-prompted gifts function in the body of Christ the way parts of a body function in a human body. Remember, in Corinth factions formed and divisions developed. Paul's letter addresses the factions by appealing to the Spirit's gifting and to God's unified purpose for the body of Christ. God designed each local church to be a place where the gifts each do their part. Together. Nothing permits us to live together well more than doing what God's Spirit calls us to do.

My mother was a soloist at times, and she was quite gifted. That's a biased accuracy. She was also at times a choir director. Even a soloist needs an instrument to be played, but when the choir cranks up its voices, we experience what many voices can do to one voice and an instrument. A Spirit-prompted gift cannot be reduced to a soloist performance. The truest expression of spiritual gifts happens when each of us does what God calls each of us to do—together. Communion occurs when there is the union in common of many. Celebrity church cultures form when gifts morph into performances on a platform resulting in fame and glory for the performer. Church happens when the gift on the platform forms into a gift given by God for the common good.

THE BODY OF CHRIST

You may have missed this. I know I did in writing up this reflection. But one of the resources I use for each passage called my attention to it. Read verse twelve again: "Just as a body, though one, has many parts, but all its many parts form one body, so it is with Christ." For some reason, I wrongly saw "the church" or the "body of Christ" ending that sentence. So, when Charles Campbell italicized *"so it is with Christ"* I saw it right (Campbell, *1 Corinthians*, 203). Paul did not say "the church." Instead, he said the one body's many parts are like *Christ*. What are we to see here? The astounding truth that Christ's body is Christ on earth today. Jesus so identifies with the church that Paul substitutes "Christ" for "church" and for "body of Christ."

Unity flows in this passage on the basis of three words: body, one, and water. The word *sōma* ("body") is used eighteen times in today's passage. A thick concentration of that word reveals emphasis. Along with that term, the word "one" appears around a dozen times. Two words make up today's reading: one and body. If God designs the church to be body-like, in fact a living, breathing, spiritual body, factions should cease. Verses twelve to fourteen articulate a theology of unity. The church is a body, not an institution, not an organization, not a collection of what-nots. Paul's image is a body and its parts. A body is a body only because its parts work together to make it work like a body. So, a church isn't a church if the members don't work together. When they don't, and let's admit this happens, the church fails to be the church.

Now to the water. Baptism locates the body's unity: "For we were all baptized by one Spirit so as to form one body—whether Jews or Gentiles, slave or free—and we were all given one Spirit to drink" (12:13). He begins with the waters of baptism. The NIV's "*by* one Spirit" could suggest the Spirit was the baptizer. The Greek term can be rendered "in" or "with," as the NIV's footnote states, which suggests believers are dipped into union with the Spirit. I prefer that sense.

Paul's switch of images from being plunged into the Spirit-waters of baptism to drinking the Spirit jars the listener. We don't drink baptismal waters! The drinking image sends us back to chapter ten and drinking from the "spiritual [or Spirit-ual] rock," who was Christ (10:4). The impact of these two watery images is unity: we all have the same baptism and the same Spirit and the same Christ.

Bodies Matter

Our physical bodies matter: "The body, however, is not meant for sexual immorality but for the Lord, and the Lord for the body" and "Do you not know that your bodies are temples of the Holy Spirit, who is in you, whom you have received from God?" (6:13, 19).

Jesus' physical body matters: "Is not the cup of thanksgiving for which we give thanks a participation in the blood of Christ? And is not the bread that we break a participation in the body of Christ?" (10:16).

> *Body of Christ matters*: "For we were all baptized
> by one Spirit so as to form one body—whether
> Jews or Gentiles, slave or free—and we were all
> given the one Spirit to drink" (12:13).

MANY, DISTINCT, NEEDED, RESPECTED PARTS

But a body's oneness is made of its many-ness (12:14). It's many-ness, however, is not just an accumulation of the same. Each body part is distinct: hands do hands, ears do ears, eyes do eyes. Not only are there many distinct parts, each part is needed. Even more, each part deserves respect for its contribution. Which means, to use Paul's body language, the parts of the body the social status crowd deems "weaker" or "less honorable" and "unpresentable" inherit an elevation in status while those parts of the body deemed by the status crowd so much are demoted to the same level as the other parts. All body parts are distinct, needed, and respected.

Paul turns his body-thinking to the church with "there should be no division" (12:25). Which suggests the body-thinking in the church led to divisions. The many parts are to have "equal concern for each other" (12:25). Noticeably, the word "concern" can mean "disturbed." Paul wants good disturbance for one another. So interrelated and needed are the many parts that "when one part suffers, all parts co-suffer" and "when one part is splendored, all parts co-rejoice" (12:26; *Second Testament*). Put simply, we are not to take delight when someone's gift is neglected, and we are all to be delighted when any gift gets the attention it deserves. "Paul keeps on trying to teach them the ironic logic of Jesus: the first shall be last, losing is gaining, turning the other cheek–all these values that directly contradict the 'logic of the world'" (Clark-Soles, *1 Corinthians*, 77).

Thinking with images helps. Let's get real. Some get to preach, others get to teach a class or group, and others are invited to play on the worship team. Our response to each can reveal our body-theology. If we are jealous over our own status and want it splendored with one of those gifts, if we are envious about someone else receiving the invitation, if we covet the beautiful exercise of a gift by another person in our fellowship, we have been Corinthian in competition about gifts. If we exercise our gift and then see someone else do the same, and we rejoice over their gift to the church, then we can unleash a cycle of co-rejoicing. If we watch someone's gift being squelched, we may witness the suffering of a sister. With her we can co-suffer.

The church is only the church when each gift is exploited for the common good, and when each member receives the gift, honors the gift as a gift from God, and rejoices over the Spirit's anointing of a brother or sister in the fellowship.

EACH WITH A PART

One more time Paul emphasizes that "each one of you is a part"—that is, the Spirit works through each of us to contribute to the body of Christ. No doubt, some had imposter syndrome or were being devalued by others or sensed their gifts were neglected. Paul pastorally extends both arms to the Corinthians to say that each person deserves equal respect for exercising a gift. I know plenty who create hierarchies of gifts: missionaries and evangelists are the top, pastors and preachers and teachers next, administrators and the so-called gift of helps come next in a descent to the least valuable. Big, bad blunder. Such hierarchies destroy unity, divide the church into the valued and disvalued, and form a culture shaped by social status. In the terms of the book of Revelation, hierarchies reveal the Babylon creep.

But Paul does numerically order gifts into first-second-third, followed by a group headed by "then" (12:28). Using numbers like this can confuse those who have just read the previous verses (12:15–26). Even more, if we are tempted to think of his numbers as a hierarchy, he contradicts what he emphasized in verse twenty-seven with the "each of you is a part." And ranking gifts may appear at the end of today's reading when Paul writes "Now eagerly desire the *greater* gifts" (12:31). I'm not sure why he numbers them, and I'm not a fan of doing so, but I do know why he put "tongues" last. That gift was causing problems because it was being used as a weapon to establish status in the church. And a suggestion that attracts me, and I hope you, is what Pheme Perkins writes. Paul's "greater" gifts is ironic because the final line "will pull the rug out from under them" by saying, "And yet I will show you the most excellent way" (12:31). Greater than even the greater gifts is love. Love knocks all gifts off their perch. Or, Boykin Sanders has another angle that levels the gifting field: "Paul does not put apostles at the top of the list to say that they rank first in the order of gifts, as some think; he puts apostles first and tongue speakers last to develop a level playing field, indeed a field wherein status and rank are no longer relevant in the building up of the body of Christ" (Sanders, *1 Corinthians*, 297).

Here's a fact. Though several people in a church may be used by the Spirit to sing or play an instrument, and several may exercise the gift of preaching or teaching, not everyone can do those gifts. So, when Paul blisters the air with those final questions—"Do all work miracles?"—the implied answer to each is *no*. Those in Corinth hearing these questions read would have encountered the gift of silence after the question was asked. Into that silence each was expected to say "No!" aloud. Such participation affirms each person in the gift assigned by God. That is the way of love.

Each with a part, and each doing her part. The church as God intended.

QUESTIONS FOR REFLECTION AND APPLICATION

1. How can a choir serve as an analogy for a well-functioning, unified church?

2. How can a human body serve as an analogy of a healthy church?

3. What other objects or structures could you use as an analogy for a church working well regarding gifts?

4. Why does love outrank all the gifts?

5. What are some differences between being jealous of another person's gifts and co-rejoicing over someone else's gifts?

LETTER ITEM #5:
GIFTS OF THE SPIRIT
(3) THE SUPERIOR PATH

1 Corinthians 13:1–13

[1] *If I speak in the tongues of men or of angels, but do not have love, I am only a resounding gong or a clanging cymbal.* [2] *If I have the gift of prophecy and can fathom all mysteries and all knowledge, and if I have a faith that can move mountains, but do not have love, I am nothing.* [3] *If I give all I possess to the poor and give over my body to hardship that I may boast, but do not have love, I gain nothing.*

[4] *Love is patient, love is kind. It does not envy, it does not boast, it is not proud.* [5] *It does not dishonor others, it is not self-seeking, it is not easily angered, it keeps no record of wrongs.* [6] *Love does not delight in evil but rejoices with the truth.* [7] *It always protects, always trusts, always hopes, always perseveres.*

[8] *Love never fails. But where there are prophecies, they will cease; where there are tongues, they will be stilled; where there is knowledge, it will pass away.* [9] *For we know in part and we prophesy in part,* [10] *but when completeness comes, what is in part disappears.* [11] *When I was a child, I talked like a child,*

I thought like a child, I reasoned like a child. When I became a man, I put the ways of childhood behind me. [12] *For now we see only a reflection as in a mirror; then we shall see face to face. Now I know in part; then I shall know fully, even as I am fully known.*

[13] *And now these three remain: faith, hope and love. But the greatest of these is love.*

Today's passage seems to interrupt the discussion of spiritual gifts. But is it an interruption, or is it a transformation of how to think about and practice the spiritual gifts? Chapter thirteen so transforms spiritual gifts that the chapter needs to be understood as the centerpiece of these three chapters. Gifts are good and varied and everybody's used by the Spirit to minister to others, but what matters most is love. In "downsizing the gifts, love reshapes, reforms, and transforms gifts from performance into spiritual formation." (Downsizing is from Sanders, *1 Corinthians*, 297.) As you read today's text you may notice that spiritual gifts come up both in 13:1–3 and in 13:8. Our chapter does not interrupt; it transforms. Transforming spiritual gifts empowers us to live together well.

The challenge for this chapter is weddings. Not in a bad sense. No, but using this chapter in weddings for the fresh love of a marriage shifts even how we read the text. In fact, some of us may be hearing music put to the words of this chapter. I stand with Charles Campbell, who wrote, "Unfortunately, the chapter has often been tamed and sentimentalized; it has been interpreted as a beautiful, inspiring idealization of marital love or individual love. Paul's words, however, are addressed to a divided community and offer a stinging critique and challenge, as well as promise, to that community" (Campbell, *1 Corinthians*, 212).

LOVE MATTERS MORE
THAN SPIRITUAL GIFTS

Four times Paul writes "If I," and what follows with each is a spiritual gift: tongues (13:1), prophecy (13:2a), faith (13:2b), and giving donations and one's body (13:3). Okay, that giving to the "poor" and surrendering one's "body to hardship" are not in any of the lists of spiritual gifts. But, if we are correct that the contribution we make to the body of Christ is our gift, we could say "giving" too is a gift. Notice that: if giving is not a gift, what is? The logic of these verses is clear: if you are exceptional in your exercise of a gift "but do not have love," you will "gain nothing" (13:3).

Love even transforms the terms Paul has used for gifts: "gifts" and "service" and "working" and "manifestation." Each of them is transformed by love into genuine actions for the "common good" (12:4–7). Maybe instead of calling them spiritual gifts we should call them love-gifts.

I have stood before many audiences. At times, the lights were so bright on the stage I could not even see most of the people. At times, I felt like a machine spitting out words to unknown people. I vastly prefer the classroom because I know my students, and for the most part, I love them. (Groans deleted.) I learned from a seasoned professor what teaching was. When I asked him, "What do you teach?" he answered, "Students, how about you?" Turning the classroom from the subject matter to the people transforms teaching into the opportunity to love. And to teach in light of love.

WHAT LOVE IS AND IS NOT

Love is and love is not shaped how Paul orders his thinking in 13:4–7. I offer my translation from *The Second Testament*, which varies enough at times in a quirky way from the NIV to become an opportunity for reflection. As you read this translation, notice how Paul moves in a chiastic manner from "Is" to "Is Not" back to "Is." That is, A—B—A.

> A: Love is: "Love patiences, love graces"
> B: Love is not: "[Love] doesn't zeal, doesn't parade oneself around, doesn't appeal to status, doesn't devalue, doesn't pursue self-matters, doesn't provoke, doesn't calculate the bad, and doesn't rejoice over wrongdoing but co-rejoices in truth."
> A: Love is: "[Love] resists all, trusts all, hopes all, is resilient in all."

These are not definitions of love but behaviors expressing love, or behaviors that don't express love. Those not expressing love (B above), may well be the sorts of behaviors that have been reported to Paul. Some of the items in B can be found in earlier parts of 1 Corinthians. Of course, each of the "love is" behaviors can be faked to weaponize them against others. Paul would know that, but his concern is to reshape how the Corinthians exercise their gifts. All he wants is for them to exercise gifts for others. He frowns on comparisons and competitions over gifts.

LOVE STAYS

Verse eight in the NIV has "Love never fails." This is a fair translation, but the Greek word, *pipto⁻*, means "fall." I have more than once wondered if someone wrote two "l's" (fall) instead of an "il" (fail), and the translation stuck. Love doesn't fall; love stays standing up. Anyway, Paul chooses the word "fall" to sum up the *permanence* of love. As he did in 13:1–3, so here: love is permanent, but the spiritual gifts of prophecy, tongues, and knowledge will "cease" or "be stilled" or "pass away" (each being similar to "fall"). People in my field (Bible, theology) need the reminder that our knowledge is "in part," an expression occurring several times in today's passage. The infinite God is ungraspable by finite human minds. We may know some things, but what we know remains only a glimpse of God.

The reason each of the gifts will "fall" is because they pertain to the "in part" or incompleteness of our time, the time between now and the final kingdom of God. The in-part-ness is like being a child while completeness is like being a mature adult (13:11). Love is permanent; it never falls, ceases, or passes away. Gifts will pass away, and that is why Paul began the passage and ended with the superiority of love.

LOVE IS SUPERIOR

Read again 12:31 and 13:13 together: "And yet I will show you the most excellent way" and "But the greatest of these is love." The passage begins and ends announcing love to be the foundation for Christian behavior. Spiritual gifts are but one form of Christian behavior. Each of the three (now classic Christian) virtues of faith, hope, and love can reshape how any spiritual gift is exercised. But of the three virtues, love is superior, or "greater" than the other two. Therefore, the way of love is superior (12:31; 13:13). Learned from Jesus (Mark 12:28–34; John 13), love formed into the very center of Christian behavior for Paul (Galatians 5:14; Romans 13:8–10). John outdoes both Jesus and Paul, using the terms more than thirty times (1 John 3:16–17, etc.).

Ecstatic experiences, special languages, the marvels of miracles, the thrill of preaching, the exhilaration of performing on stage on Sunday morning in a megachurch, the pride in seeing your name in print—none of these compares to the fundamental Christian virtue of love. Love matters, all else falls.

QUESTIONS FOR REFLECTION
AND APPLICATION

1. How does the context into which Paul wrote this passage differ from the contexts in which it is most often used today?

2. Why does love matter so much for the usage of gifts in the church?

3. Randomly pick five of the behaviors that love does or doesn't do and go through the list of gifts in 12:8–10 or 12:28 reflecting on how that behavior impacts that gift.

4. What difference does the translation "fall" versus "fail" make for you?

5. Why will gifts end? Why won't love end?

LETTER ITEM #5:
GIFTS OF THE SPIRIT
(4) GIFTS IN WORSHIP

1 Corinthians 14:1–25

[1] *Follow the way of love and eagerly desire gifts of the Spirit, especially prophecy.* [2] *For anyone who speaks in a tongue does not speak to people but to God. Indeed, no one understands them; they utter mysteries by the Spirit.* [3] *But the one who prophesies speaks to people for their strengthening, encouraging and comfort.* [4] *Anyone who speaks in a tongue edifies themselves, but the one who prophesies edifies the church.* [5] *I would like every one of you to speak in tongues, but I would rather have you prophesy. The one who prophesies is greater than the one who speaks in tongues, unless someone interprets, so that the church may be edified.*

[6] *Now, brothers and sisters, if I come to you and speak in tongues, what good will I be to you, unless I bring you some revelation or knowledge or prophecy or word of instruction?* [7] *Even in the case of lifeless things that make sounds, such as the pipe or harp, how will anyone know what tune is being played unless there is a distinction in the notes?* [8] *Again, if the trumpet does not sound a clear call, who will get ready for battle?* [9] *So it is with you. Unless you speak intelligible words with your tongue, how will anyone*

know what you are saying? You will just be speaking into the air. [10] Undoubtedly there are all sorts of languages in the world, yet none of them is without meaning. [11] If then I do not grasp the meaning of what someone is saying, I am a foreigner to the speaker, and the speaker is a foreigner to me. [12] So it is with you. Since you are eager for gifts of the Spirit, try to excel in those that build up the church.

[13] For this reason the one who speaks in a tongue should pray that they may interpret what they say. [14] For if I pray in a tongue, my spirit prays, but my mind is unfruitful. [15] So what shall I do? I will pray with my spirit, but I will also pray with my understanding; I will sing with my spirit, but I will also sing with my understanding. [16] Otherwise when you are praising God in the Spirit, how can someone else, who is now put in the position of an inquirer, say "Amen" to your thanksgiving, since they do not know what you are saying? [17] You are giving thanks well enough, but no one else is edified.

[18] I thank God that I speak in tongues more than all of you. [19] But in the church I would rather speak five intelligible words to instruct others than ten thousand words in a tongue.

[20] Brothers and sisters, stop thinking like children. In regard to evil be infants, but in your thinking be adults. [21] In the Law it is written:

> "With other tongues
>   and through the lips of foreigners
> I will speak to this people,
>   but even then they will not listen to me,
>   says the Lord."

[22] Tongues, then, are a sign, not for believers but for unbelievers; prophecy, however, is not for unbelievers but for believers. [23] So if the whole church comes together and everyone speaks in tongues, and inquirers or unbelievers come in, will they not say that you are out of your mind? [24] But if an unbeliever or an inquirer comes in while

everyone is prophesying, they are convicted of sin and are brought under judgment by all, [25] *as the secrets of their hearts are laid bare. So they will fall down and worship God, exclaiming, "God is really among you!"*

In the 1970s, the charismatic movement was for all the cool kids. I wanted to be part of the group. I wanted to speak in tongues. I tried a few times by getting myself prepared. I jacked myself up. Once or twice, on my knees, Bible before me, I went before the Lord, opening my mouth in the hope of tongue-speaking. Nothing happened. When my jaw tired out, I closed up shop and went back to doing what I was going to do. I've never spoken in tongues. I'm open to it. I no longer think it's for the cool kids. It's for those whom the Lord chooses. There is not a hint in the New Testament that tongue-speaking was only for the first century church. Tongue-speaking, distributed as it is by the Spirit, is for whenever the Spirit wants it to occur.

Tongue-speaking was divisive in the '70s, as it was divisive in the '50s in Corinth. Divisiveness was a major issue in Corinth (see Introduction, pp. 1–16). Supernatural actions that are more or less spiritual but unintelligible attract those seeking experiences. They certainly did me. Tongue-speaking is no sign of super-spirituality. If anything, the obsession with tongues in Corinth went hand in hand with a messed-up group of believers. Some in Corinth used tongue-speaking as a weapon against those whom they deemed less spiritual. Competition wounded the assemblies. It still does. When we approach any spiritual gift, including tongues, through the pastorally wise advice of 1 Corinthians 12 and exercise all gifts in love according to 1 Corinthians 13, we end up with the kind of wisdom found in 1 Corinthians 14. Thirteen reshapes twelve, leading into the wisdom of fourteen.

In public worship, when the church is assembled, some gifts will be more displayed than others. Paul believes the most significant gift in the public assembly of the church is prophecy. He believes everyone has a gift; he believes every gift is valuable and each person valued; but he believes prophecy contributes to the whole assembly. That's what today's passage seems to teach. Let's dig in a bit. Paul compares prophecy to tongues in this passage. We take them one by one, starting with tongues. (Remember, too, that when Paul asks questions, he expects the audience to answer them aloud.)

TONGUES

There is much confusion about tongues, so I want to offer a clear reading of what Paul says about tongues. For some, it may be a fresh reading. I have, you may already be muttering to yourself, set for myself a nearly impossible task. But with your permission, I want to give it a go.

To begin with, Paul both speaks in tongues himself and wishes all could speak in tongues (14:5, 18). Thus, Paul offers himself as an example of someone who *could* speak in tongues publicly but, evidently, chooses not to. (It can be done.) What concerns Paul most is that tongue-speaking, when uninterpreted, edifies or forms only the tongue-speaker (14:4, 6). Gifts are not for self-edification when done in the assembly. God designs gifts for the formation of all, that is, for the common good (12:7). One catches here a hint, if only a hint, of the high-status people speaking in tongues and using the gift to claim special status among the believers.

Tongue-speaking is Spirit-prayer and Spirit-singing (14:15; the NIV has lower case "spirit" and adds the word "my"). When done privately or publicly tongue-speaking can express thanksgiving (14:17). Paul compares tongue-speaking to note-less sounds, and says it is unintelligible like an unknown language (14:7–8, 9, 10–11, 16, 19).

Which is why Paul insists, when they are gathered, that tongue-speaking should only occur if it is publicly interpreted so it can be formative for all (14:5, 13). Interpretation, so it appears to me, can be done by either the tongue-speaker or by someone else (12:10; 14:5, 13). The aim of tongue-speaking is "Amen," the Aramaic word for expressing solidarity with what was said. Tongue-speaking, when interpreted, can become "some revelation or knowledge or prophecy or word of instruction" (14:6). But I agree with Pheme Perkins that the "upshot . . . is to suppress tongues-speaking in communal worship" (Perkins, *First Corinthians*, 158).

Thinking of tongues as capable of transcending one's ability to speak in a language one does not know, Paul's mind goes back to a passage that must have played an important role in the church from Pentecost on. In Isaiah 28 the prophet says God will speak to the people "with other tongues and through the lips of foreigners," which instead of astounding the people of God into attentiveness, they ignore (1 Corinthians 14:21). Which leads Paul to comment then that God designed (at least some sorts of) tongue-speaking to be foreigners speaking to the people of God. This at least could be one way of understanding what happened at Pentecost (Acts 2). As such, tongues-speaking was a "sign for unbelievers," which was designed by God as judgment on the people of God (1 Corinthians 14:21–22).

When in the assembly, however, if novices or even unbelievers are present—house churches could not avoid this in most cases—they will be confused by any sort of tongue-speaking (14:16, 23). If you feel tension between this and the previous two verses, I join you. I believe the previous two verses are about Pentecost and not the same as what Paul describes in 14:23. In 14:24–25 Paul says the words of a prophet, being intelligible, can work redemption in novices and unbelievers.

PROPHECY

If tongue-speaking refers to a kind of ecstatic speech, prophecy entails (1) revelation from God, (2) spoken by a prophet, (3) to the people of God, (4) for their spiritual formation. As such, prophetic words are revelations that lead to reformation of the people of God. To begin today's passage, Paul exhorts us both to "Chase love" and also to "be zealous for the Spirit-prompted gifts" (14:1; *Second Testament*). He adds a vital word after "Spirit" when he writes "especially prophecy." In saying "especially" he begins his comparison with tongue-speaking.

Prophecy's value for the church is that it is formational, and he uses three terms to express this: "strengthening, encouraging and comfort" (14:3). Because prophecy is intelligible to all (14:9, 19), it is "greater than . . . tongues" (14:5). However, if tongue-speaking is interpreted, and then becomes a word of prophecy or revelation or instruction or knowledge, then prophecy would not be deemed "greater."

Prophecy can have a dual function. The fundamental idea of prophecy is God revealing to a prophet a message for the people of God. That is, Israel, Judah, or the church. The prophets Isaiah and Jeremiah had words for and about the nations around them, but they were speaking more *about* than *to* these people. The same applies here: the gift of prophecy comes from God to the church and for the church's formation, both at the personal and corporate levels. As such, a newspaper columnist or a blogger who tosses their words onto the waves of the public are not acting prophetically. Which must be softened: at times, such public words speak to the people of God prophetically.

The second function of prophecy concerns novices or unbelievers in the assembly. Some Jewish synagogues were on the city square and could have had traffic or visitors attending. The churches of Corinth were most likely apartments or villas. Unbelieving people could be present. Unbelieving business associates could make a visit. Unbelieving renters or dependents may well have attended the assemblies. Paul instructs them not to be speaking in tongues but to utter words of prophecy. Unbelievers may become convinced and the inner world overturned by the prophecies. Paul knew from experience that such persons may fall down uttering the confession that "God is really among you!" (14:25; sounds like either Isaiah 45:14 or Zechariah 8:23).

GUIDEPOSTS

Paul offers four guideposts for exercising spiritual gifts. First, a negative one: he rebukes them for their immaturity in saying "stop thinking like children" (14:20; cf. 3:1–2; 13:11). Their childlikeness, instead of Christlikeness, pertains to comparing gifts and competing for the more supernatural gifts. Adulting contents oneself with the gift God has assigned to each of us. Second, Paul urges all over again that the way forward in all public exercise of gifts is the way of love (13:1–13; 14:1). He urges each of them to be zealous for Spirit-prompted gifts (14:1), especially prophecy. Paul thinks all can be used by God to speak prophetically. One writer calls this the "prophethood of all believers" (Campbell, *1 Corinthians*, 232). Whatever the gift, their design must be clarified and lived into: they're designed by God for spiritual formation of the community. The words in the NIV are "edifies" (14:3–5) and "build up" (14:12), but these NIV words translate the same Greek word. The fundamental question for the one exercising a gift is, "How will this help to form someone spiritually?"

I give it an everyday example. Kris just walked in our back door from purchasing a few items at our farmer's market. She had a story. As she arrived, she came upon a rather fierce argument between a white woman and two Asian women. The white woman was angry at the two women. She accused them of bumping her car in the parallel parking slots in front of a local church. There were no signs of any bump. The Asian women denied it. Kris stepped into the situation and asked the two Asian women, "How can I help?" They proceeded to explain their side of the story. The white woman interrupted with her side of the story. A handy policeman was near. He defused the situation, asking again what was going on. Accusations flew back and forth. The policeman pointed out that the white woman had gone well beyond her parking spot's borders, the white woman more or less got angry, got in her car, and in a huff drove away. What Kris did (and what the policeman did) illustrate the essence of what a spiritual gift does: it asks, "How can I help?" The help is the spiritual gift.

QUESTIONS FOR REFLECTION AND APPLICATION

1. What have been your experiences with tongue-speaking, or what teachings have you heard on the topic?

2. How does the gift of prophecy compare with the gift of tongues?

3. What is the difference between how adults handle gifts and how children handle gifts?

4. What role do gifts play in the spiritual formation of people in the church?

5. How do you feel called to help others in the church?

LETTER ITEM #5:
GIFTS OF THE SPIRIT
(5) ORDERLY WORSHIP

1 Corinthians 14:26–40

26 *What then shall we say, brothers and sisters? When you come together, each of you has a hymn, or a word of instruction, a revelation, a tongue or an interpretation. Everything must be done so that the church may be built up.* 27 *If anyone speaks in a tongue, two—or at the most three—should speak, one at a time, and someone must interpret.* 28 *If there is no interpreter, the speaker should keep quiet in the church and speak to himself and to God.*

29 *Two or three prophets should speak, and the others should weigh carefully what is said.* 30 *And if a revelation comes to someone who is sitting down, the first speaker should stop.* 31 *For you can all prophesy in turn so that everyone may be instructed and encouraged.* 32 *The spirits of prophets are subject to the control of prophets.* 33 *For God is not a God of disorder but of peace—as in all the congregations of the Lord's people.*

[34 *Women should remain silent in the churches. They are not allowed to speak, but must be in submission, as the law says.* 35 *If they want to inquire about something, they should ask their own*

husbands at home; for it is disgraceful for a woman to speak in the church.]

³⁶ *Or did the word of God originate with you? Or are you the only people it has reached?* ³⁷ *If anyone thinks they are a prophet or otherwise gifted by the Spirit, let them acknowledge that what I am writing to you is the Lord's command.* ³⁸ *But if anyone ignores this, they will themselves be ignored.*

³⁹ *Therefore, my brothers and sisters, be eager to prophesy, and do not forbid speaking in tongues.* ⁴⁰ *But everything should be done in a fitting and orderly way.*

At times, someone contends churches would be better if there were no pastors, or at least no paid pastors. Such persons contend we need to gather and let happen what the Spirit wants to happen. The irony of having, to use typical language, no one in charge means the ones who don't want someone being in charge are actually in charge. Such persons want chaos and anarchy to rule. They want disruptions. I have joked over the years—and it's not really a joke—that leaderless churches last about a month. Someone quickly, however gently and wisely, rises into guidance for the group. Evidently in Corinth the anarchists were in charge. They wanted an assembly that had no rules, no order. Just a free-for-all. Paul had learned that when the anarchists take over, the church falls apart. So, he offers three bits of wisdom for conducting orderly assembly meetings.

---

* Many today think Paul did not write 14:34–35. The reasons include that (1) early manuscripts reveal hesitations about these verses being by Paul; some things don't sound like Paul (women were prophesying and praying in Paul's churches; there is nothing in the law of Moses that sounds like silence and submission of women in public assemblies; some women were teaching in the early churches). Others think these verses are interruptive comments by opponents of Paul (see my note in *The Second Testament*, at p. 188).

ORDERLY WORSHIP

First, assemblies are designed front, left, and center for formation: "Everything must be done so that the church may be built up" (14:26). I offer a caution here. Gathering to *learn* from a sermon is not always the same as formation. Formation is measured over time by transformation, not by information.

Second, Paul urges orderliness when he says, "God is not a God of disorder," and he contrasts that with "peace." Paul saw in their anarchy of these gatherings conflicts and tensions rather than peace (14:33). The word Paul uses for disorder is *akatastasia*, a word suggesting instability and chaos. God does not do anarchy. God does the "fitting and orderly way" (14:40). The Greek word for "orderly" is *taxis*, and it refers to an organized manner, a structure, or a system. *Get yourself an order for worship, let it shape your time together, but permit Spirit-prompted moments of spontaneity.* What Paul writes here becomes an orderly service by the second century. Justin Martyr describes an early Christian assembly (*First Apology*, 67):

> On the day which is called Sunday we have a common assembly of all who live in the cities or in the outlying districts, and the memoirs of the Apostles or the writings of the Prophets are read, as long as there is time. Then, when the reader has finished, the president of the assembly verbally admonishes and invites all to imitate such examples of virtue. Then we all stand up together and offer up our prayers, and, as we said before, after we finish our prayers, bread and wine and water are presented. He who presides likewise offers up prayers and thanksgivings, to the best of his ability, and the people expressed their approval by saying "Amen." The Eucharistic elements are distributed and consumed by

those present, and to those who are absent they are sent through the deacons. The wealthy, if they wish, contribute whatever they desire, and the collection is placed in the custody of the president. [With it] he helps the orphans and widows, those who are needy because of sickness or any other reason, and the captives and strangers in our midst; in short, he takes care of all those in need.

We are not to think this describes precisely what Paul wanted done in Corinth, but it does describe *generally* the orderliness of the early church's gatherings. This order of worship sounds very much like the liturgy of today's liturgical churches. If you'd like to see what one looks like, open *The Book of Common Prayer* to what is called a Eucharistic worship service (see link after the reflection questions). All the liturgical churches—Roman Catholic, Anglican, Episcopalian, Methodist, Presbyterian, Lutheran, American Baptist—have adopted and adapted the basic order of the text above from Justin Martyr. Again, "as in all the congregations of the Lord's people," though we'd have to modify it to "in most of the congregations."

Third, he pushes for solidarity or communion with other churches. When he says, "as in all the congregations of the Lord's people" (14:33), he's informing that order is the way the people of Jesus worship. Paul gets worked up at this point to ask two pointed questions: "Or did the word of God originate with you? Or are you the only people it has reached?" (14:36). That is, a kind of edgy *Who do you think you are to vary from all the churches we have formed?* Perhaps it was less edgy. Something like *This orderliness is the way the people of Jesus gather.* The free-for-all in Corinth, which Paul describes as disruptive, disorderly anarchy, is not the way of the churches of Jesus.

SOME RULES TO FOLLOW

Orderliness for tongue-speaking looks like these basic rules:

For tongues:

1. No more than three tongue-speakers.
2. One at a time. Tongue-speakers don't talk over one another or interrupt.
3. There must be an interpreter.
4. If there is no interpreter, speak in tongues at home (14:27–28).

For prophets:

1. No more than three prophets speaking.
2. Everyone should listen with discrimination.
3. If someone gets a prophetic revelation while one is speaking, the first prophet sits down and gives the voice to the one with revelation.
4. Prophets speak in turn, not at the same time.
5. Prophecy is for the purpose of forming apprentices and encouragement.
6. Prophets are governed by prophets (14:29–32).

Paul urges the Corinthians to "be eager to prophesy" and yet, also, "do not forbid speaking in tongues" (14:39). It is not a little discomforting that most churches today are so orderly no one prophesies (but the preacher, if he or she does) and very few permit public tongue-speaking. Put more forcefully, they have turned away from both of Paul's bits of wisdom here. Both. Underline that.

I'm a person of order, and I like these words of Paul. Some of my friends, and I am not qualified to diagnose their personality type, prefer the free-for-all. What Paul's churches reveal is an orderliness that is also open to the spontaneous. He wants the use of all the gifts in an orderly way. As he says to open today's reading, "When you come together, each of you has a hymn, or a word of instruction, a revelation, a tongue or an interpretation" (14:26). This can't happen in a megachurch. Paul's idea of a church was a house church.

All the gifts, all the time, in an orderly manner. That's how we are to live together in a way that unites the church.

QUESTIONS FOR REFLECTION AND APPLICATION

1. Why is orderliness important for worship meetings?

2. What do you think of Justin Martyr's description of an early church gathering?

3. In what ways was the church in Corinth not following principles of orderliness?

4. Do you prefer a set liturgy in church or a more spontaneous and flexible service?   .

5. How do you think orderliness could enhance the practice of using gifts in church?

FOR FURTHER READING

The Book of Common Prayer: https://www.bcponline
.org/. Click on "The Holy Eucharist." Then "The
Holy Eucharist: Rite II" then click on the same
words on the page that appears, and there it is!
Justin Martyr, *First Apology*, in *The Fathers of the
Church 6: St. Justin Martyr*, trans. Thomas B.
Falls (Washington, D.C.: Catholic University
Press of America, 1948).

LETTER ITEM #6: RESURRECTION (1) THE GOSPEL OF RESURRECTION

1 Corinthians 15:1–11, 20–28, 42–58

¹ Now, brothers and sisters, I want to remind you of the gospel I preached to you, which you received and on which you have taken your stand. ² By this gospel you are saved, if you hold firmly to the word I preached to you. Otherwise, you have believed in vain.

³ For what I received I passed on to you as of first importance: that Christ died for our sins according to the Scriptures, ⁴ that he was buried, that he was raised on the third day according to the Scriptures, ⁵ and that he appeared to Cephas, and then to the Twelve. ⁶ After that, he appeared to more than five hundred of the brothers and sisters at the same time, most of whom are still living, though some have fallen asleep. ⁷ Then he appeared to James, then to all the apostles, ⁸ and last of all he appeared to me also, as to one abnormally born.

⁹ For I am the least of the apostles and do not even deserve to be called an apostle, because I persecuted the church of God. ¹⁰ But by the grace of God I am what I am, and his grace to me was not without effect. No, I worked harder than all of them—yet not I, but the grace of God that was with me. [11] Whether, then, it is I or they, this is what we preach, and this is what you believed.

[20] *But Christ has indeed been raised from the dead, the firstfruits of those who have fallen asleep. [21] For since death came through a man, the resurrection of the dead comes also through a man. [22] For as in Adam all die, so in Christ all will be made alive. [23] But each in turn: Christ, the firstfruits; then, when he comes, those who belong to him. [24] Then the end will come, when he hands over the kingdom to God the Father after he has destroyed all dominion, authority and power. [25] For he must reign until he has put all his enemies under his feet. [26] The last enemy to be destroyed is death. [27] For he "has put everything under his feet." Now when it says that "everything" has been put under him, it is clear that this does not include God himself, who put everything under Christ. [28] When he has done this, then the Son himself will be made subject to him who put everything under him, so that God may be all in all.*

[42] *So will it be with the resurrection of the dead. The body that is sown is perishable, it is raised imperishable; [43] it is sown in dishonor, it is raised in glory; it is sown in weakness, it is raised in power; [44] it is sown a natural body, it is raised a spiritual body.*

If there is a natural body, there is also a spiritual body. [45] So it is written: "The first man Adam became a living being"; the last Adam, a life-giving spirit. [46] The spiritual did not come first, but the natural, and after that the spiritual. [47] The first man was of the dust of the earth; the second man is of heaven. [48] As was the earthly man, so are those who are of the earth; and as is the heavenly man, so also are those who are of heaven. [49] And just as we have borne the image of the earthly man, so shall we bear the image of the heavenly man.

[50] *I declare to you, brothers and sisters, that flesh and blood cannot inherit the kingdom of God, nor does the perishable inherit*

the imperishable. *51* *Listen, I tell you a mystery: We will not all sleep, but we will all be changed—52 in a flash, in the twinkling of an eye, at the last trumpet. For the trumpet will sound, the dead will be raised imperishable, and we will be changed.* *53* *For the perishable must clothe itself with the imperishable, and the mortal with immortality.* *54* *When the perishable has been clothed with the imperishable, and the mortal with immortality, then the saying that is written will come true: "Death has been swallowed up in victory."*

> *55* *"Where, O death, is your victory?*
> *Where, O death, is your sting?"*

56 *The sting of death is sin, and the power of sin is the law.* *57* *But thanks be to God! He gives us the victory through our Lord Jesus Christ.*
58 *Therefore, my dear brothers and sisters, stand firm. Let nothing move you. Always give yourselves fully to the work of the Lord, because you know that your labor in the Lord is not in vain.*

Today's reading is the first of five separable units in the famous resurrection chapter of 1 Corinthians 15. Separable, but not unconnected. The gospel of the resurrection, which appears in three parts, forms the heart of the chapter. Responsive to the audience that he is, the apostle Paul interrupts his description of the gospel two times to answer questions. He knows his audience would ask these questions at the very moment he inserts them (cf. 15:12, 29–30, 32, 35). So, the order of the chapter looks like this:

The gospel of the resurrection, part one (15:1–11)
    Question (15:12–19)
The gospel of the resurrection, part two (15:20–28)
    Questions (15:29–41)
The gospel of the resurrection, part three (15:42–58)

What Paul separates we will bring back together! The reasons for looking at them together are two-fold: first, because we tend to ignore the resurrection in our understanding of the gospel and, second, because we will then discover the breadth of the gospel itself. Today's reflection concerns the three parts of the gospel of resurrection. The next one turns to the questions the Corinthians had about resurrection.

The heart of the circle of the gospel is a person: God (in three persons). Surrounding the heart is the resurrection, and surrounding the resurrection is the crucifixion and burial, and surrounding the crucifixion and burial is the life (teaching, actions, etc.) of Jesus. As we approach the circle, we encounter the person of Jesus, and the deeper we go into Jesus, the closer we get to the life and death and resurrection of Jesus. In proceeding through these circles, we encounter God, the God who reveals himself in the face of Jesus Christ.

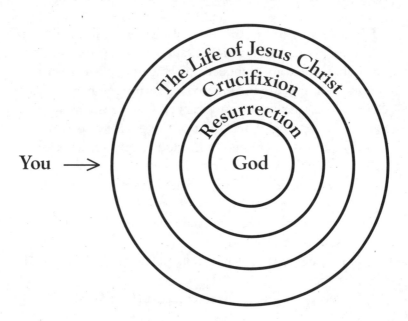

PASS IT ON

Take a look at verse three: "What I received" is the gospel, and what he received he "passed on" to the Corinthians. He received the gospel from Jesus himself (Galatians 1:11–12), but the gospel he received from Jesus was confirmed by the apostles (1:13–24). From Jesus, confirmed by his close apostles—that's what Paul passed on. This gospel from Paul the Corinthians "received," they "have taken [their] stand" on it, they are "saved" by it, and they have "believed it" (1 Corinthians 15:1, 2, 11).

Paul's gospel is *the* gospel, not just *his* gospel. We know this because of the sermons in the book of Acts (Acts 2:14–39; 3:12–26; 4:8–12; 10:34–43; 11:4–18). Paul preached the same gospel (13:16–41; 14:15–17; perhaps 17:22–31). Peter and Paul thus flesh out the outline of the basics Paul states in 1 Corinthians 15:3–5. We know this, also, because the four Gospels flesh out even more than what we read in 1 Corinthians 15:3–5 and the sermons in Acts. The Gospels tell the fullest gospel story of the entire New Testament. The gospel then can be reduced to four events in the life of Jesus himself: that "Christ died for our sins" and that "he was buried," and that "he was raised," and that "he appeared" (15:3–5). This story about Jesus is "according to the Scriptures" (15:3, 4). This story about Jesus redeems because the Subject of the story is the Savior, Jesus.

Paul becomes self-conscious when he describes the gospel. He knows that the fourth chapter in the gospel is about the appearances of Jesus, and he knows Jesus appeared to him on the road north to Damascus, but he knows he didn't deserve an appearance from Jesus. So, he says, "I am the least of the apostles" (15:9), and that is only by the "grace of God" that he is what he is—saved and propelled by God's Spirit into a life of telling the Roman world about Jesus (15:10–11).

Gospelers, or evangelists, today need to return to the gospel. We have too many tricksters and manipulators whose primary skill is telling emotive stories backed up by organ music or a worship band's soft tunes. Too many rely on their own skills. Too many rely on the fear of death and final punishment (hell). There is not one word about final punishment in this gospel summary in 1 Corinthians. It's all about Jesus—his life and death and burial and resurrection. And salvation and forgiveness from sins. But the gospel is the story *about* Jesus, and not what we get out of it. Too many gospelers today are good talkers about what we get but not enough talk about Jesus. Paul's gospel tells people about Jesus. The gospel is the foundation for our life together.

Gospeling today tells people about Jesus. The evangelistic question of all questions can be reduced to one: "Who do you think Jesus is?" Or, "What do you think of Jesus?" Gospelers faithful to the gospel lead people to Jesus, and in Jesus, people discover and experience redemption, liberation, salvation, justification, and reconciliation. Into a new life with Jesus and those who love him.

"ALL IN ALL"

The second gospel passage is found in 15:20–28. The theme of these verses is not heard often enough when we talk gospel in churches. The gospel tells a story of Jesus that not only saves us but also eventually utterly and completely destroys death. The enemy is death. Once Jesus has conquered and destroyed "all dominion, authority and power," he will hand over the entire cosmos to the Father so that "God may be all in all."

Our gospel is not big enough. The story it tells is not big enough. We have shrunk to the individual, to the individual's present redemption and future destiny. But the gospel of Paul is cosmic, cosmic, cosmic. The powers of this world, all bent toward death and domination, will be defeated by the Son of God. Redemption in Jesus, then, is caught up in a cosmic battle between God and the systemic powers of this world ruled by Satan. The story about Jesus, according to 15:20–28, reveals then that Jesus has entered into this world to live and die and to be raised *as the means of conquering sin, systemic evil, and Satan,* all so Jesus the Son of God can hand over a "Mission Accomplished" package called Planet Earth to the Father—so God, who is the heart of the gospel itself, can be who God is: "all in all."

You know why children and adults love *The Lord of the Rings* or *The Chronicles of Narnia?* You know why they love Homer's *Iliad* and *The Odyssey?* Or Virgil's *The Aeneid?* Or Dante's *The Divine Comedy?* Or Milton's *Paradise Lost?* Or Bunyan's *The Pilgrim's Progress?* Because those stories are so big, their lens so broad, and their soul so deep. They do not settle for one character, say Frodo or Lucy, being saved. They don't settle until their entire universe has been liberated, evil eliminated, and the truth and justice and peace are established.

And God is "all in all." All creation's purpose is to bend toward and before God, to bring God glory. At times we get so wrapped up in the *saving benefits* of the gospel we make the gospel about us and what we get out of it. In theological terms, that's idolatry. The famous Westminster Catechism, which I will update in language, begins its question-and-answer format with "What is our chief end?" The answer is "Our chief end is to glorify God and to enjoy him forever." When "end" means "ultimate, final, and eternal purpose" we stand next to 1 Corinthians 15:28: God is "all in all." God will be our full desire, our deepest delight, and our fathomless knowledge.

TAUNTING DEATH

The true enemy of God, of the gospel, of Jesus is death. Our enemy is death. Death destroys. Elizabeth Strout, a wonderful novelist, offers this scene of a reflection on death:

> He told how his father had died while he was on the train coming back from San Francisco. "What I didn't know about death," Tyler said, squinting at his fingernails, "was that it was not just the death of my father, but the death of my childhood, the death of the family as I'd known it. It reminds me of Glenn Miller's plane disappearing above the channel. Not just the death of a bandleader, you see, but the death of a band." He looked out the window. "That's what death does. If that makes any sense." (*Abide with Me*, 81)

Because of those often unanticipated ever-widening powers of death, I love to hear, whether in scripture read or in song, Easter music. The greatest line ever penned about Easter, however, was a taunt by the apostle Paul. His taunt is both a proclamation and an application: "Where, O death, is your victory? Where, O death, is your sting?" (15:55). The gospel that conquers death is the cosmic gospel of all cosmic gospels. Death is the driving aim of sin, of systemic injustices, and of Satan. The victory of God occurred on Easter Day about 33 AD. The gospel's inner circle is the resurrection because it both swallows the death of Jesus and turns it inside out into a cross that leads to the victory of the resurrection.

Paul's gospel story has an either-or framing:

Perishable	Imperishable
Dishonor	Glory
Weakness	Power

Natural	Spiritual
Living being	Life-giving spirit
First Adam	Second Adam
Earth	Heaven
Image of earthly man	Image of the heavenly man
Flesh and blood	
Mortality	Immortality

In column one you find the problem the gospel about Jesus resolves; in column two we discover the multiple dimensions of salvation and redemption in the gospel.

Percolating through this entire passage is the theme of the body. The bodies we have will be redeemed. The resurrection does not mean our souls are released from physical captivity. The body will experience in the resurrection, not its destruction, but its transformation into a body like that of Jesus after his resurrection. As Beth Felker Jones reminds us, "When death is finally no more, we will be shaped entirely by the love of God embodied in Jesus Christ. Finally, our bodies are for praise, praise of the one who is victor over death, who will shape us into witnesses to beauty, to goodness, to holiness, and to peace" (Jones, *Marks of His Wounds*, 112).

Disabilities will be undone. The social stigmas of disabilities, which have endlessly plagued those with disabilities, will be shown for the evil they are, lamenting and repenting will occur, and social status will be healed and redeemed. Aging will be reversed. Each of us will be the body God designed us to be. (I discuss the questions people ask about heaven in *The Heaven Promise*, part four.) None of these symptoms of the system of death will be left as they are because death will not have the last word. The last word will be "all in all," and the All-in-All will release life into our bones and blood, and we will live eternally in the glory of God's kingdom. Not up in heaven, but in a kingdom on a redeemed earth filled with redeemed bodies. Bodies matter to the gospel.

STAY PUT

The practical implications of the gospel of the resurrection wait until the last verse of fifty-eight! "Stay put!" is one way to translate it. He wants them to stick to the resurrection, to the gospel that defeats the cosmic powers behind death. In sticking to the gospel, they are to live a life of "flowing over in the Lord's work." Their resurrection gospel provides the conviction that their "labor isn't hollow in the Lord" (15:58; *Second Testament*). In the next passage we reflect on why this "stay put" is important: the Corinthians had some very serious questions about the resurrection, and some of what they were pondering could easily corrupt the entire gospel.

I conclude with this: the gospel is bigger than the four spiritual laws. The gospel, to be faithful to the words of Scripture, must be cosmic to become fully personal. We can live our best life with that massive gospel.

QUESTIONS FOR REFLECTION AND APPLICATION

1. Why does Paul insert questions and answers into his gospeling?

2. How did Paul receive the gospel he passed on?

3. What are the four events that make up the core of the gospel?

4. What are the differences between a gospel message that talks about what we get and a gospel that talks about Jesus?

5. List some of your favorite epic stories. What elements of them echo the good news found in the gospel?

FOR FURTHER READING

Beth Felker Jones, *Marks of His Wounds* (New York: Oxford, 2007).
Scot McKnight, *The Heaven Promise* (Colorado Springs: WaterBrook, 2015).
Elizabeth Strout, *Abide with Me* (New York: Random House, 2007).

LETTER ITEM #6: RESURRECTION (2) QUESTIONS ABOUT THE RESURRECTION

1 Corinthians 15:12–19, 29–41

12 But if it is preached that Christ has been raised from the dead, how can some of you say that there is no resurrection of the dead? 13 If there is no resurrection of the dead, then not even Christ has been raised. 14 And if Christ has not been raised, our preaching is useless and so is your faith. 15 More than that, we are then found to be false witnesses about God, for we have testified about God that he raised Christ from the dead. But he did not raise him if in fact the dead are not raised. 16 For if the dead are not raised, then Christ has not been raised either. 17 And if Christ has not been raised, your faith is futile; you are still in your sins. 18 Then those also who have fallen asleep in Christ are lost. 19 If only for this life we have hope in Christ, we are of all people most to be pitied.

29 Now if there is no resurrection, what will those do who are baptized for the dead? If the dead are not raised at all, why are people baptized for them? 30 And as for us, why do we endanger

*ourselves every hour? ³¹ I face death every day—yes, just as surely
as I boast about you in Christ Jesus our Lord.*

*³² If I fought wild beasts in Ephesus with no more than human
hopes, what have I gained? If the dead are not raised,*

> *"Let us eat and drink,
>   for tomorrow we die."*

*³³ Do not be misled: "Bad company corrupts good character." ³⁴
Come back to your senses as you ought, and stop sinning; for there
are some who are ignorant of God—I say this to your shame.*

*³⁵ But someone will ask, "How are the dead raised? With what
kind of body will they come?" ³⁶ How foolish! What you sow does
not come to life unless it dies. ³⁷ When you sow, you do not plant
the body that will be, but just a seed, perhaps of wheat or of something else. ³⁸ But God gives it a body as he has determined, and to
each kind of seed he gives its own body. ³⁹ Not all flesh is the same:
People have one kind of flesh, animals have another, birds another
and fish another. ⁴⁰ There are also heavenly bodies and there are
earthly bodies; but the splendor of the heavenly bodies is one kind,
and the splendor of the earthly bodies is another. ⁴¹ The sun has one
kind of splendor, the moon another and the stars another; and star
differs from star in splendor.*

One of the features of Paul's letters are his Q&A's.
Because readers tend to read the questions and quickly
move on, in *The Second Testament*, Paul's questions are put in
bold font with answers to the questions immediately under
them. Paul was a church-planting missionary who constantly
faced the questions of new believers. These new believers
came from a variety of backgrounds. The questions reflected
that kind of variety, too. Today's reading combines two sections of 1 Corinthians 15. Both sections are Q&A's that have
interrupted Paul's articulation of the gospel.

Frankly, most of us have questions about the resurrection, or at least about what happens to us after we die. The Christian belief is that when we die, we become immediately conscious of being present with God. (The alternative is called "soul sleep," which means we are unconscious until the resurrection.) But at the general resurrection, when Jesus has conquered all evil and all principalities and powers, we will be raised with a kingdom, heavenly body fit for the eternal kingdom of God. We will have a body; the kingdom will be a renovation of planet earth when heaven joins earth; we will know who we are, and we will fellowship with others in an eternal, vibrant life—where each day is new and better. We will be known, and we will know. We will continually grow in being all God made us to be. (See my book, *The Heaven Promise*.)

QUESTION #1

Paul's first question reflects, as all four do, what some in Corinth believed and asked. His question basically reveals the logical inconsistency of some: if the gospel requires the resurrection, then "how can some of you say that there is no resurrection of the dead?" (15:12). Remember that resurrection for Paul (and most Jews) was about a body being made fit for the Age to Come or the kingdom of God. Paul responds to the inconsistency with a string of "*if-then*" statements, and I will reformat them and fill in some blanks to see both how the three premises (A, B, C) work and how they work by repetition toward a conclusion. It's a bit complicated but what makes it complicated are mostly Paul's repetitions.

A1: If there is no resurrection of the dead,
      then not even Christ has been raised (15:13).

B: If Christ has not been raised,
    [Then] our preaching is useless and
    [Then] so is your faith [useless].
    [Then] More than that, we are then found to be
        false witnesses about God, for we have testified
        about God that he raised Christ from the dead
        (15:14–15).
A2: But . . . if in fact the dead are not raised,
    [Then] *he did not raise him* (15:15 end).
A3: For if the dead are not raised,
    then Christ has not been raised either (15:16).
B2: If Christ has not been raised,
    [Then] your faith is futile;
    [Then] you are still in your sins
    Then those also who have fallen asleep in Christ
        are lost (15:17–18).
C: If only for this life we have hope in Christ,
    [Then] we are of all people most to be pitied
        (15:19).

How to summarize these repetitive but intense logical moves? The premise of the whole gospel and this chapter is *God raised Jesus from among the dead ones.* This is stated or assumed in 15:13, 15. The second move turns toward the gospel preaching: Paul preaches *the gospel of Jesus' resurrection.* The third move shifts into the implications if this gospel and this resurrection are untrue. The entirety of the Christian faith rests upon the bodily resurrection of Jesus and that same faith utterly collapses if there is no resurrection. What falls apart is (1) the resurrection of Christ, (2) the gospel preaching, (3) their faith, (4) they become false witnesses, (5) they are still in their sins, and (6) Christians are pitiful for believing in such a silly idea.

If Jesus was buried in a shallow grave, as some have

contended, or if Jesus remained in the tomb, then there is no gospel in Jesus. If there is no resurrection, Jesus was little more than an inspiring, idealistic prophet who met an unjust end. If Jesus was not raised by God, then I've wasted my adult life on gospel preaching and teaching. God forms the center of the gospel, and the next concentric circle is the resurrection (pp. 210). It all collapses if the resurrection circle goes blank.

Thus, if some in Corinth don't believe in a bodily resurrection, then they are not Christians. The gospel of God's grace for us rests on raising the body of Jesus out of a grave by an act of God.

QUESTION #2

A doubled question now is raised about "those who are baptized for the dead": (1) "what will those do who are baptized for the dead?", and (2) "If the dead are not raised at all, why are people baptized for them?" (15:29). Contained by one verse, these two questions, and what some think they imply as early Christian practice (baptizing for those already dead), this verse has set off a rhizome of roots, branches, leaves, blossoms, and shade for what lurks under them. First, notice the question is about *the ones being baptized* not about (1) the ones for whom they are baptized or (2) what happens to the ones for whom they are baptized. Thus, *those who are baptized* and *why are people baptized for them?*

Second, we don't know what these Corinthians believed. We can infer they thought being baptized for those already dead who probably had not believed (mistakenly) procured their salvation.

Third, Paul uses this mistaken practice to establish a more important point: If they are being baptized for those who are dead, *then they must think (1) there is a resurrection, and (2) it will procure redemption and is thus at the heart of the Jesus-gospel.* In other words, once again, their practice baptism flies in the face of their claim that there is no such thing as a resurrection of the body.

QUESTION #3

The third question turns personal for Paul, and it too is a doubled question—"Why do we [gospel agents] endanger ourselves every hour?" along with, "If I fought wild beasts in Ephesus with no more than human hopes, what have I gained?" (15:30, 32). The first is answered in 15:31, the second in 15:32b–34. Paul lived a life on the edge of death—every day he faced opposition that could spark the fire of persecution and could have led to death. Notice that Paul uses the term "boast" in 15:31, where he boasts about the Corinthians. In 2 Corinthians 11:21–33 he connects that same term to his persecutions. He lists his sufferings in his mission work for churches. In 1 Corinthians 15:30–34 he contends he suffers because of his hope in the resurrection. *But if there's no resurrection, why bother?* That's how Paul thinks.

It appears Paul blames associates for this theological error—"Ignorant of God" (15:34)—of denying the resurrection when he quotes Menander's saying, "Bad company corrupts good character" (15:33).

QUESTION #4

The fourth question is yet another doubled question: "But someone will ask, 'How are the dead raised? With what kind of body will they come?'" (15:35). One has to guess on the basis of what we know about the ancient world to know what's happening in these questions. The major view is that some in Corinth thought like Plato. They thought the body was bad and the soul good. That death liberated the soul from the body to experience an eternal soul-freedom. Paul was Jewish. Paul was Christian. The Christian Jew, Paul, believed like most Jews that *resurrection meant a real body, however transformed*. To quote what Tom Wright has said over and over. Resurrection is more than belief in life after death. Resurrection is a life after life after death! (Wright, *Surprised by Hope*).

Paul believes the body given to each of us is designed for the world in which we live. There is a present world, in which the kingdom has been launched, and a future world, in which the kingdom will be fully realized.

A Roman View of Death

The turncoat Josephus, in Rome, rehearses a very Roman/Greek understanding of what happens at death in a speech by the military leader, Titus, son of the emperor Vespasian, during the Jewish war with the Romans:

As for myself, I shall at present waive any commendations of those who die in war, and omit to speak of the immortality of those men who are slain in the midst of their martial bravery; yet cannot I forbear to imprecate upon those who are of a contrary disposition that they may die in time of peace, by some distemper or other, since their souls are already condemned to the grave, together with their bodies; for what man of virtue is there who does not know that those souls which are severed from their fleshly bodies in battles by the sword, are received by the ether, that purest of

---

elements, and joined to that company which are placed among the stars; that they become good demons and propitious heroes, and show themselves as such to their posterity afterwards? While upon those souls that wear away in and with their distempered bodies, comes a subterranean night to dissolve them to nothing, and a deep oblivion to take away all the remembrance of them, and this, notwithstanding they be clean from all spots and defilements of this world; so that, in this case, the soul at the same time comes to the utmost bounds of its life, and of its body, and of its memorial also; but since fate hath determined that death is to come of necessity upon all men, a sword is a better instrument for that purpose than any disease whatsoever. Why, is it not then a very mean thing for us not to yield up that to the public benefit, which we must yield up to fate? (Josephus, *War* 6.46–49; Whiston)

The kingdom body follows the death of the present body. Paul illustrates with seeds that must die to form a "body" designed by God in its maturation. Much like a butterfly emerges from the death of the caterpillar to be regenerated through chrysalis formation, leading then to the closing of the butterfly. Bodies are shaped for each form of life: people, animals, birds, and fish. Noticeably, there is also for humans an earthly and a heavenly body (15:40). And there is a splendor or glory for each: sun, moon, and stars.

Here, Paul sketches the difference between our earthly body and our heavenly body (as noted in Question #4). We will be given a body fit for the kingdom. Recognizable from its earthly body, the heavenly body will transcend the earthly body.

Earthly Body	*Heavenly [Kingdom] Body*
Perishable	Imperishable
Dishonor	Glory
Weakness	Power
Natural	Spiritual
Living being	Life-giving spirit
First Adam	Second Adam
Earth	Heaven
Image of earthly man	Image of the heavenly man
Flesh and blood	
Mortality	Immortality

So, back to the question, "With what kind of body will they come?" The second column reveals precisely his answer. With a body fit for the eternal kingdom of God. That body will be like the resurrected body of Jesus we read about in Matthew 28, Luke 24, and John 20–21. And Revelation 1!

Here are pastoral words from Jaime Clark-Soles, words I love: "Resurrection takes death seriously; Platonism does not. Resurrection says Death is real, not an illusion. Death is sad and painful—even the best deaths. Death may dog us, try to drag us down into hopelessness and loneliness and fear, *and yet* it does not have the last word, its days are numbered, and its defeat is sure" (Clark-Soles, *1 Corinthians*, 108).

But, only if the resurrection of Jesus happened.

QUESTIONS FOR REFLECTION
AND APPLICATION

1. What have you previously been taught and believed about the resurrection and heaven?

2. Why is a belief in the bodily resurrection of Jesus so central to the gospel?

3. How were Jewish beliefs different from Roman beliefs about the body?

4. How do you feel about the idea of having a renewed and resurrected real human body living on a new earth after death?

5. How do you think cremation and organ donation fit with Paul's view of the resurrection and the kingdom body?

FOR FURTHER READING

Scot McKnight, *The Heaven Promise* (Colorado Springs: WaterBrook, 2015).

N. T. Wright, *Surprised by Hope* (New York: HarperOne, 2008).

The Works of Flavius Josephus, Complete and Unabridged, New Updated Edition, translated by William Whiston, A.M. (Peabody, MA: Hendrickson Publishers, 1987).

LETTER ITEM #7:
THE COLLECTION

1 Corinthians 16:1–4

[1] *Now about the collection for the Lord's people: Do what I told the Galatian churches to do.* [2] *On the first day of every week, each one of you should set aside a sum of money in keeping with your income, saving it up, so that when I come no collections will have to be made.* [3] *Then, when I arrive, I will give letters of introduction to the men you approve and send them with your gift to Jerusalem.* [4] *If it seems advisable for me to go also, they will accompany me.*

Togetherness was Paul's primary motive for his decades-long collection of funds for the poor believers in Jerusalem. You can read about this collection in numerous places in Paul's letters, including Galatians 2:1–10, today's passage and 2 Corinthians 8–9, and Romans 15:14–32. Paul persuaded most of the churches in his mission to support his collection. For Paul the collection embodied the unity of the churches, both Jewish and gentile, both Petrine mission churches and Pauline mission churches (Galatians 2:1–10). Noticeably, for the Jerusalem churches to receive Paul's collection risked the safe standing of churches in a city nervous about Paul's rumored lack of concern with law observance.

One has to wonder if that is why Luke does not mention the collection when he gets to Jerusalem (cf. Acts 21:17–26), and maybe Luke has called it "alms" in 24:17 in order to cool some of the heat about Paul.

WHAT TO CALL IT?

Paul called his collection various terms, including a grace gift (1 Corinthians 16:3; 2 Corinthians 8:6), a blessing (9:5), a liturgy or a "public work's service" (9:12; *Second Testament*), a service (Romans 15:31; 1 Corinthians 16:15; 2 Corinthians 8:4), and a fellowship or "making resources common" (Romans 15:26; *Second Testament*). There is much to ponder in the use of such different terms. Each term explores how believers live together even when they disagree at times.

Churches Contributing to the Collection

Galatia (1 Corinthians 16:1)
Derbe, Lystra, Berea, Thessalonica (Acts 16:1; 20:4)
Macedonia (2 Corinthians 8:1–5; 9:2, 4)
Philippi (Acts 16:12, 16; 20:6)
Corinth (Romans 15:26)
Mysia, Ephesus (Acts 20:4)

REMEMBER

This collection was for those who were poor. Christians inherited from their Jewish Bible and the practices of Judaism the use of their material resources for the good of the poor. In this they were distinguished from most of the Roman world where the poor languished and died or wrestled life from meager resources. If we factor in Galatians 2:10, Acts 11:27–30, Romans 15:26, and 2 Corinthians 8–9, there can be no doubt Paul's collection was for the poor, and the term for "poor" in this instance refers to the destitute driven to begging. Every Christian living consistently with the gospel, and we can see this especially in 2 Corinthians 8–9, generously contributes somehow to those in need. It is our inheritance as Bible-shaped believers. Paul urges that believers in Corinth, instead of cramming at the last minute, set aside money each week (1 Corinthians 16:2). The collection would be taken to Jerusalem. With Paul, at least in his plans, would be representatives from each church who would be accompanied with hearty letters of affirmation by Paul himself (16:3).

GENEROSITY: GOOD AND NOT SO GOOD

Generous donations for others can express a variety of motives but more importantly it embodies some Christian virtues, like compassion, unity across the churches, worship of God in thanksgiving for what God provides, and equality between believers (see McKnight, *Pastor Paul*, 86–99). The church's budget can be measured for its compassion, unity, equality, and worship quotients by how much of its resources is used to help those in need.

Generosity can express the exuberant compassion of the one with resources, but for the recipient, it may be a painful reminder of poverty, not belonging, and otherness. Calvin Miller, reflecting on his own past, offers words we all need to keep in mind whenever and every time we donate to the poor:

> Needless to say, we children didn't want to go to those churches that brought us the baskets. The last place you

want to go worship is the place where the people need you to be poor so they themselves can feel rich in the dispensation of their charity. There is something grandiose about giving a beggar a dime, but there is nothing grandiose in receiving it. Beggars don't ask for money so they can think well of themselves, but because feeling bad about themselves is usually less painful than starvation. (Miller, *Life Is Mostly Edges*, 58–59)

Which is why Jesus said, "do not let your left hand know what your right hand is doing" (Matthew 6:3).

There is a time for donors to reveal themselves, and it looks a lot like a later experience in Miller's life. You may need a tissue.

"Now, I remember you," he said. "You received two hundred and fifty dollars as a special gift from someone. With this money you brought in, your tuition is paid for the year."

. . . I just thought it was my old Franciscan lookalike, Brother Daley. But I was wrong about it being him. For two decades I pondered over the anonymous offering, without which I might not ever have finished college, and my entire future would have been altered.

Twenty years later at my mother's funeral, while I stood at her graveside grieving my loss, an old man I barely knew approached me. Claude Simons is his name if ever you should want to celebrate his presence in heaven. The old man had always been an old man. He lived alone and he had never been anything more than a floor-sweep at the Pillsbury Mill. Still, had every soul been as noble as he, the gates of Eden would never have clanged shut. He walked up to me even as I wept, put his arms around my heaving shoulders, and patted me on the chest with his frail old hand. "Dr. Miller," he said softly, but with a twinkle in his eye, "did you ever wonder where that two hundred and fifty dollars came from on your second year at OBU?" "I've wondered all my life," I told him. "I gave it," he said. "And by the way, you were worth every penny of it . . . and then some." In such moments I forgive the church for sometimes being so unlike its Founder, and remember that here and there Jesus is right: the meek still inherit the earth. (Miller, *Life Is Mostly Edges*, 118–119)

Amen.

QUESTIONS FOR REFLECTION AND APPLICATION

1. For whom was Paul collecting funds?

2. Why was Paul collecting this offering?

3. How was Christian generosity different from that of the surrounding Roman culture?

4. Is your church's budget measured by its compassion? If that became the driving force for budgetary decisions, how would that change things?

5. When have you received financial support? What did it mean to you?

FOR FURTHER READING

Scot McKnight, *Pastor Paul* (Grand Rapids: Brazos Press, 2019).
Calvin Miller, *Life Is Mostly Edges* (Nashville: Thomas Nelson, 2008).

PLANS

1 Corinthians 16:5–24

⁵ After I go through Macedonia, I will come to you—for I will be going through Macedonia. ⁶ Perhaps I will stay with you for a while, or even spend the winter, so that you can help me on my journey, wherever I go. ⁷ For I do not want to see you now and make only a passing visit; I hope to spend some time with you, if the Lord permits. ⁸ But I will stay on at Ephesus until Pentecost, ⁹ because a great door for effective work has opened to me, and there are many who oppose me.

¹⁰ When Timothy comes, see to it that he has nothing to fear while he is with you, for he is carrying on the work of the Lord, just as I am. ¹¹ No one, then, should treat him with contempt. Send him on his way in peace so that he may return to me. I am expecting him along with the brothers.

¹² Now about our brother Apollos: I strongly urged him to go to you with the brothers. He was quite unwilling to go now, but he will go when he has the opportunity.

¹³ Be on your guard; stand firm in the faith; be courageous; be strong. ¹⁴ Do everything in love.

¹⁵ You know that the household of Stephanas were the first converts in Achaia, and they have devoted themselves to the service of the Lord's people. I urge you, brothers and sisters, ¹⁶ to submit to

such people and to everyone who joins in the work and labors at it.
¹⁷ I was glad when Stephanas, Fortunatus and Achaicus arrived,
because they have supplied what was lacking from you. ¹⁸ For they
refreshed my spirit and yours also. Such men deserve recognition.

¹⁹ The churches in the province of Asia send you greetings.
Aquila and Priscilla greet you warmly in the Lord, and so does the
church that meets at their house. ²⁰ All the brothers and sisters here
send you greetings. Greet one another with a holy kiss.

²¹ I, Paul, write this greeting in my own hand.

²² If anyone does not love the Lord, let that person be cursed!
Come, Lord!

²³ The grace of the Lord Jesus be with you.

²⁴ My love to all of you in Christ Jesus. Amen.

The ends of Paul's letters are as tempting to skim for the reader as they are for the one writing about them! But in these endings, we often read details we'd never know otherwise. We hear about three men who must have been sent by Paul and who probably carried this letter to Corinth and read it aloud. We catch a glimpse of where Paul is (Asia, which means Ephesus), and who is with him. But this letter has something quite special. It tells us more about how Paul planned, or didn't plan, than any place in all his letters.

OPEN TO THE LORD'S GUIDANCE

There are two in our household. When we plan on a trip this is how it works when it works best: one of us comes up with the idea. In our older years, we have been able to afford some special trips to places I have always wanted to visit. Here's one: Naxos, an island in Greece. I came up with the idea, Kris took care of the details. Like airplane tickets. Flying to the islands requires skills we have had to learn. We plan to drive around an island but don't plan minute-by-minute.

We wing it if we want. We decide in the moment at times where to lunch and where to have dinner.

I take some kind of wink-wink delight in reading about Paul's plans in 16:5–12. I italicize expressions that left the Corinthians baffled at what Paul was actually going to do. Notice these:

> After I go through Macedonia, I will come to you.
> Perhaps I will stay with you for a while, or even spend the winter.
> So that you can help me . . . wherever I go.
> I hope to spend some time with you.
> If the Lord permits.
> I will stay on at Ephesus until Pentecost.

At this point the Corinthians may have muttered "until Pentecost or sooner or later. Who knows what he might do!"

> When Timothy comes . . . Send him on his way in peace so that he may return to me . . . I am expecting him along with the brothers.

Translated more literally, the opening "when" is "if" and that little "if" changes the whole paragraph into "what will happen will happen."

> Apollos . . . I strongly urged him to go to you with the brothers. He was quite unwilling to go now, but he will go when he has the opportunity.

Apollos, as we have observed earlier in this letter, was the BFF for some of the Corinthians but Paul's not entirely clear either about the man's willingness to go back to Corinth or, when he does go, when that will happen.

What to learn. First, I'm so glad he wrote this section. It shows he was open to the Lord's guidance while simultaneously making plans. He was ready to go and ready to be interrupted by a prompting of the Spirit. He didn't have a rigid schedule but a free spirit. It's hard at times to work with people like this. Plans at times get in the way of the Lord's work. Once in motion, the Lord can redirect us or keep us on the original path. Some people know what they are called to do from their teenage years, and others make several career-shifting adjustments. Nearly every student I now teach in the seminary is a second- or third-career person. Becky Castle Miller, who skillfully writes the questions at the end of these reflections, came to our seminary to be formed more deeply for pastoral work—where she learned to write such good questions! Once at Northern Seminary, however, she discovered her joy in academic work and is now doing a PhD in New Testament studies. On emotions, which shows her pastoral calling. She may end up teaching, she may end up pastoring. Like Paul, we'll see!

UNITY

The "first converts in Achaia" (Greece) were the "household of Stephanas," who then discovered his calling in the ministry of serving others (probably a deacon; 16:15). Faithful folks like him deserve respect by the Corinthians. With that, and Paul uses the term I translate as "order yourselves under" him, Paul returns to the theme of unity. Listening to one's leaders doesn't mean doing whatever one wants, but it does mean, well, a measure of conformity. Leaders who claim this verse's sense of spiritual authority are usually those who are guilty of spiritual abuse of power, but leaders who are worthy of their calling do receive respect and orderliness from their people. People who want power are problems. People who gain respect from others are not the problem. To sound like Paul, I add *in most cases* and *usually* and *as long as the will of God is done.*

Paul was thrilled when Stephanas along with Fortunatus and Achaicus, the latter two probably freed slaves and perhaps employed by Stephanas, got to Ephesus with some generous contributions ("supplied what was lacking from you" and "refreshed my spirit and yours also") as well as some reports and news, both good and bad.

The network formed through travel and letters expresses the unity Paul wants between himself and the Corinthians. Paul formed this network so they could live together and work on uniting this divided church. He has five directions that can heal some divisions and form some unities: "Be on your guard; stand firm in the faith; be courageous; be strong. Do everything in love" (16:13–14). But it takes time to turn a divided church into a unified church.

GREETINGS

Greetings are passed on from the "churches in the province of Asia" (look at Revelation 2–3 for the locations of churches in that area), from Aquila and Priscilla, the church in their home, and from "all the brothers and sisters here" (16:19–20). The Corinthians, as the letter was being read, would have smiled here and there about those they knew and did not know. One can glimpse a gleam of unity in these greetings.

Paul closed the letter with his own handwriting because he relied on others with better penmanship to write his letters (16:21).

Out of the blue he erupts with a sudden curse on those who don't love the Lord. His famous *maranatha,* "Our Lord come," of 16:22 may well be a prayer for the Lord to come in judgment on sin. A rather sudden, if not disappointing, ending to a letter. Which is chased down and away with a prayer for the grace of God to be upon them, as well as with an expression of his love for all of them (16:23–24). Good words for an ending for a letter filled with tumultuous relations.

QUESTIONS FOR REFLECTION AND APPLICATION

1. What is the big-picture idea of Paul's plans?

2. What can we learn about Paul from such planning and closing sections of his letters?

3. Why are flexible plans important for people in ministry?

4. How does Paul reemphasize his theme of unity in this closing?

5. At the conclusion of 1 Corinthians, reflect on what you have learned about this letter. What most stands out to you?

New Testament Everyday
Bible Study Series

Become a daily Bible reader attentive to the mind of God

In the New Testament Everyday Bible Study Series, each volume:

- offers brief expositions of the biblical text and offers a clear focus for the central message of each passage;
- brings the passage alive with fresh images and what it means to follow King Jesus;
- provides biblical connections and questions for reflection and application for each passage.

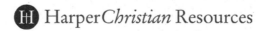

GREAT BOOKS

ARE EVEN BETTER WHEN THEY'RE SHARED!

Help other readers find this one

- Post a review at your favorite online bookseller

- Post a picture on a social media account and share why you enjoyed it

- Send a note to a friend who would also love it—or better yet, give them a copy

Thanks for reading!

The Blue Parakeet, 2nd Edition

Rethinking How You Read the Bible

Scot McKnight, author of
The Jesus Creed

How are we to live out the Bible today? In this updated edition of *The Blue Parakeet*, you'll be challenged to see how Scripture transcends culture and time, and you'll learn how to come to God's Word with a fresh heart and mind.

The gospel is designed to be relevant in every culture, in every age, in every language. It's fully capable of this, and, as we read Scripture, we are called to discern how God is speaking to us today.

And yet applying its words and directions on how to live our lives is not as easy as it seems. As we talk to the Christians around us about issues that matter, many of us wonder: how on earth are we reading the same Bible? How is it that two of us can sit down with the same Bible and come away with two entirely different answers about everything from charismatic gifts to the ordaining of women?

Professor and author of *The King Jesus Gospel* Scot McKnight challenges us to rethink how to read the Bible, not just to puzzle it together into some systematic belief or historical tradition but to see it as an ongoing Story that we're summoned to enter and to carry forward in our day.

What we need is a fresh blowing of God's Spirit on our culture, in our day, and in our ways. We need twenty-first-century Christians living out the biblical gospel in twenty-first-century ways. And if we read the Bible properly, we will see that God never asked one generation to step back in time and live in ways of the past.

Through the Bible, God speaks in each generation, in that generation's ways and beckons us to be a part of his amazing story.

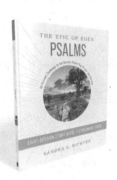
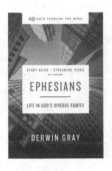
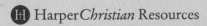

Following King Jesus

We want to follow King Jesus, but do we know how?

Author and professor Scot McKnight will help you discover what it means to follow King Jesus through 24 lessons based on four of his writings (*The King Jesus Gospel*, *The Blue Parakeet – 2nd edition*, *One.Life*, and *A Fellowship of Differents*). McKnight's unique framework for discipleship is designed to be used for personal study and within disciple-making groups of two or more. In this workbook, McKnight will help you:

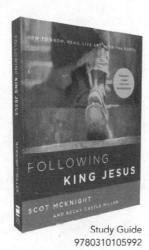

Study Guide
9780310105992

- Know the biblical meaning of the gospel
- Read the Bible and understand how to apply it today
- Live as disciples of Jesus in all areas of life
- Show the world God's character through life together in the church

Each lesson, created by Becky Castle Miller, has both Personal Study and Group Discussion sections. The Personal Study section contains a discipleship reading from Scot McKnight, an insightful Bible study, an insightful Bible study, and a time for individual prayer, action, and reflection. The Group Discussion section includes discussion questions and activities to do together with a discipleship group. You'll share insights from your personal study time with each other and explore different ways of living out what you're learning.

Whether you have been a Christian for many years or you are desiring a fresh look at what it means to be a disciple, this workbook is an in-depth guide to what it means to follow King Jesus and to discover how to put that kind of life into practice.

Harper*Christian* Resources